The Forty-First

Ypres

THE FORTY-FIRST

Being a Record of the 41st AIF
during the Great War

Members of the Intelligence Staff

The Naval & Military Press Ltd

Published by
The Naval & Military Press Ltd
5 Riverside, Brambleside, Bellbrook
Industrial Estate, Uckfield, East Sussex,
TN22 1QQ England
Tel: +44 (0) 1825 749494
Fax: +44 (0) 1825 765701
www.naval-military-press.com
www.military-genealogy.com
www.militarymaproom.com

In reprinting in facsimile from the original, any imperfections are inevitably reproduced and the quality may fall short of modern type and cartographic standards.

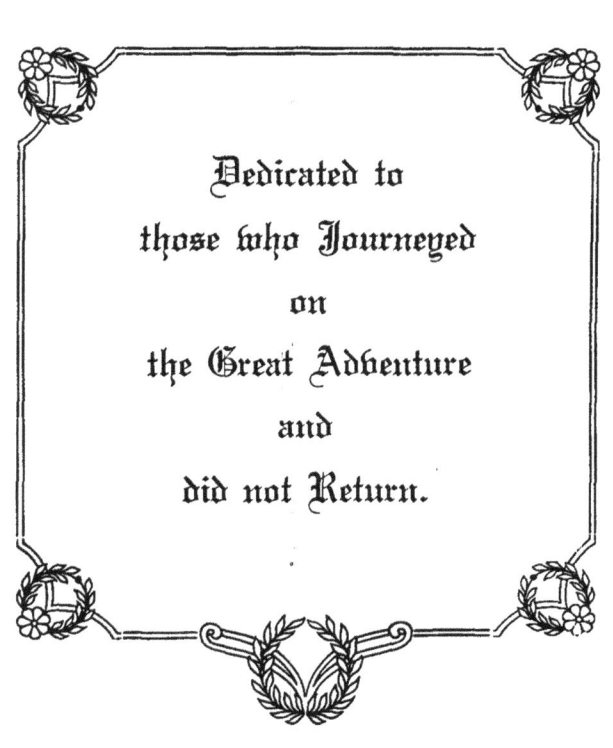

Dedicated to
those who Journeyed
on
the Great Adventure
and
did not Return.

FOREWORD.

By Brig.-Genl. Jas. H. Cannan, C.B., C.MG., D.S.O.

After the fighting on Somme of 1916 it was with great pleasure I learned that I was to assume command of the 11th Australian Infantry Brigade, of which 41st Battalion formed part.

This book is the work and effort of certain members of the 41st Battalion, and all of these members took part in the operations of that unit, hence the book fairly well records the glorious work done by the 41st, and forms an historical record for those who have friends or relatives of members who took such a glorious part in the magnificent exploits of 41st. It is to the credit of 41st Battalion that they never lost a prisoner to the enemy, which is a unique record.

To every member of 41st Battalion the book will be an interesting souvenir, and a reference to its pages will ever help to remind them of the happy associations and important incidents surrounding their life whilst fighting for King and Empire in the Great War of 1914-1919.

JAS. H. CANNAN,
Brigadier-General.

PREFACE.

The following pages make no pretence at being a military treatise of the War from a battalion point of view, such as would cause unfortunate schoolboys of a later generation to place ice on their foreheads whilst their brains performed acrobatic feats grappling with strategical problems.

Moreover it is not claimed as the modern "Decline and Fall of the German Empire." What is aimed at, is a souvenir in print which will aid the old blue and black oval "digger" when holding forth to an open-eyed and admiring family, data to spur him on to further flights of (alas!) fancy.

It is unnecessary to mention that nobody but the Intelligence Section—who although perhaps wanting in literary attainments is not lacking in pluck—cared to tackle the proposition. Even they found it more difficult than "faking" information, losing the battalion, or, as in some isolated cases, dishing up the "dinkum oil."

If the book awakens recollections of stirring fights, days of misery or nights at cafés (which you never told the wife about), in fact, can keep you from falling asleep over your pipe, then our object is attained.

F. W. M.

St. Maxent, France,
   30th December, 1919.

Working Party — Messines 1917.

PHASE I.

CHAPTER I.

Formation of 41st Battalion, A.I.F.—Training at Bell's Paddock.—May, 15, 1916, Departure for Sydney.—On board the Demosthenses.—Life at Sea.—Cape Town.—Crossing the Line.—St. Vincent.—Madeira.—Devonport.—First Impressions of England.—Larkhill Camp.—Training and Snow.—November 24th and 25th.—Crossing to France.—Le Havre.—Railway Journey to Bailleul.—Some Impressions of the French.—March to Armentieres.

At the beginning of 1916 it was thought possible by the Military Authorities that a Queensland Brigade could be formed, equipped, and despatched to the front, before the second half of the year. In accordance with this scheme, four battalions were formed in the 1st Military District in and about Brisbane in January. The battalion then stationed at Bell's Paddock Camp, Brisbane, was known as the 35th Battalion. Owing to a fall in the rate of enlistments, the project had to be abandoned, and two battalions only were formed; the 35th becoming the 41st.

As far as possible, members of the two remaining nuclei were absorbed into these battalions, so that towards the end of February the personnel of the 41st Battalion was complete, comprising men from Metropolitan, North Queensland, and Northern Rivers (New South Wales) areas. Subsequent reinforcements to the battalion, however, represent the whole of Queensland.

After January, and until the date of departure from camp, elementary training gradually gave way to battalion training, when full battalion movements were carried out.

Specialists, such as machine-gunners, signallers, and bombers received special training at Rifle Range Camp in their particular classes of work.

By May 15, every member of the battalion was fully equipped and had passed the usual efficiency tests, received final home-leave, and had practice at the grand old recreation, so much in vogue at the front, route-marching.

On the evening of May 15th all members of the battalion celebrated, each as he thought fit, the eve of our departure for the front, and next morning at a very early hour the battalion was "fallen in" for the last time on the old parade ground, and after breakfast marched to the Rifle Range Station, entraining there for Sydney, the port of embarkation.

Colonel Halstead, who commanded at Bell's Paddock, came to see us off, and received unmistakeable evidence of his popularity with the " boys," as the train moved out.

The Battalion Headquarters Staff personnel at this period were Lieut.-Colonel F. J. Board, commanding, with Major J. Milne as second in command, and Lieut. C. S. French as Adjutant.

As is usual when a battalion receives movement-orders, an advance party had been sent on ahead to make preparations, and to see to the loading of battalion stores.

Throughout the train journey patriotic bodies assembled at halting places, providing eatables and hot drinks, and indeed all along the line evidence that we were leaving old " Aussie " with the heartiest good wishes of all was not wanting.

The main body reached Sydney on the evening of the 17th, and after a short march through the by-ways of the city embarked on the steamer " Demosthenes."

That night, hammocks, blankets, and mess kits were issued, and the companies were made acquainted with the particular regions they were to occupy as mess and sleeping quarters during the voyage.

There were on board, besides the 41st Battalion, the first reinforcement of the 41st Battalion, a Cyclist Company, Sanitary Detail A.A.M.C., and 13th Divisional Supply Unit (29th A.A.S.C.), with several officers of the 11th Brigade Infantry Staff.

The ship carried a war-cargo of wheat, wool, frozen meat (including rabbits), and hides.

At 2 p.m. next day the journey began. The course kept us in sight of land as far as Bass Strait. Thereafter we saw no land until Albany, our first port of call, was reached. As we continued south, the weather became colder and the sea rougher, and the pitching and rolling of the vessel soon picked out the sailors amongst us. The novelty of the situation, the study of the sea and its denizens, and speculation on the identity of many headlands seen in the distance, helped to settle us and reconcile us to our cramped quarters.

From Bass Strait through the Bight to Albany the voyage was exceedingly rough and the cold intense, so that the majority of us kept below. That passage through the Bight to Albany was a horrible nightmare to many of us, and it was a profound relief to get even a few hours' rest at Albany. We coaled here, and the canteen-stores were augmented. It was hoped that a chance of exercising on shore would be given us, but as another transport was already at the wharf, we anchored out in mid-harbour and coaled from lighters. This completed, we again got under weigh.

Ours was a most mysterious voyage. Everywhere could be heard whispers about "Sealed Orders," and uncertainty as to the course we were to take opened up great possibilities in entirely new lines of navigation—a source of keen amusement to the ship's officers. It was only when several days had passed that the sun threw light on a riddle by setting daily straight ahead of us. We then realised that there was a considerable stretch of sea between us and the next land, and the true significance of the term "all at sea" dawned on us. Also Christopher Columbus received a meed of praise that would have been most flattering to him could he have been there to hear it.

During the first part of the trip, from Australia to the Cape, the rough weather impeded training and exercise to a considerable extent. However, nobody had much to complain about in crossing the Indian Ocean, as by that time the Bight had cured us of any mal-de-mer we might otherwise have experienced. Training consisted for the most part of physical drill and rifle-exercises. Many of us had not yet got our "sea legs" and consequently occasioned much merriment. Mess orderlies found it particularly trying to maintain equilibrium in narrow passages and on the stairways, and we were often treated to the amusing sight of one of them well-plastered with the food he had tried to carry to his mess, that is, when it was not our own mess. At night, too, the hammocks, never at any time what could be described as stable, were constantly bumping their occupants together, and it became a feat even to climb into them. Moreover, one's hammock never seemed to remain long in the spot where it was stored each morning. It must have been that some hammocks were superior to others, for every man was issued with one.

Off parade, the time was passed in recreation, such as reading, and games of all kinds. The game of "house" soon became the most popular on the boat, and one could not go to any part of the deck without hearing the chant of the proprietor of an outfit.

Besides such recreations as our resourcefulness provided, boxing matches and concerts were arranged and held weekly, and never failed to "draw" well.

We were fortunate in having something to "grouse" about. This time it was the food, which was neither as plentiful nor as well-cooked as that to which we had been accustomed in camp in Australia, and it was only that sense of discipline for which the battalion was later to become famous that prevented certain dark threats which had been levelled at the cooks from being carried out. The limited amount of fresh water was one of the chief reasons for the insipid taste of the food. However, the Canteen came to the rescue, and each time a few cases of tinned fruit, biscuits, chocolates, &c., were opened at the canteen, about half the battalion lined up. That is where we learned to stand in queues, a common enough thing in later days.

When two days off the Cape a wireless was received conveying the sad tidings of the death of Lord Kitchener. A Memorial Service was held, and was attended by all on board, including those of the ship's officers and crew who were not on duty.

The towering plateau of Table Mountain and pinnacled ridge of the Twelve Apostles at length came into view, or rather would have, had not a phenomenally dense fog settled down over sea and land just as the Cape was sighted on the evening of June 19th. We entered Table Bay at nightfall, with the yellow flag flying at the masthead, a sight which cast a shadow of gloom upon us all.

Our stay lasted nine days, and no leave was granted, but those who could afford to pay for a tour on shore assured their mates that Cape Town was a very fine place and the people very hospitable. Several route-marches were held, and one day was devoted to football and athletic sports, held at Green Point, a name that has many historical associations. We could not remain at the wharves all the time we were in port, so the anchor was dropped about half-a-mile from shore. Every day, whilst daylight lasted, we were besieged by a crowd of merchants, white and black, who offered for sale the small souvenirs chiefly in demand by troops. Most of the men took advantage of the opportunity to collect views of the town and other souvenirs, and lay in stocks of oranges, which seemed to be the only fruit in season at that time in Cape Town. Incidentally they were taken advantage of by the coloured merchants, who showed irritating inconsistency in their charges. A shilling bought twelve oranges, a penny four, and a half-penny two or three. The exchange was effected through the medium of baskets let down by strings, secured to the rail in case of accident.

The hospitality of the people of Cape Town knew no bounds. If a company went on a route march, all along the streets of town and suburbs the inhabitants ran out of their houses to greet the " boys " as they passed, and showered gifts of oranges upon them, whilst the Mayoress raised a collection of a hundred pounds to buy comforts for them. Some, more fortunate than the rest, " fell on their feet " straight away, making friends with members of the opposite sex, which in many cases resulted in a mutual correspondence lasting for years.

To those who had no money to spare Cape Town lost all attraction by the ninth day, especially as the fortunate ones who returned daily, in small parties in various small craft, gave glowing accounts of the time they had in the city. Indeed so loath were they to leave it that it is regrettable to record that compulsion was necessary to get all on board in time for leaving the port. In order to realise fully the expensive nature of these shore trips, we would add that motor-launches often cost as much as five pounds a time.

After leaving the Cape, the weather became perceptibly warmer each day and the seas less rough, and from that time onward, many began to take their first interest in life at sea. By this time everyone knew that our destination was England, and not Egypt or India, and we began to look forward to our arrival in the land of our forefathers, and to make plans accordingly.

At Cape Town we became one of a fleet of five, the other vessels being our convoy, an auxiliary cruiser named "Laconia," and three other transports, "Warilda," "Medic," and "Ascanius." It is interesting to note that it was the sinking of the "Laconia" that finally brought America into the war. Those liable to prostration when the seas were rough, envied the men in the "Medic," which was a very long boat, and on that account seemed less likely to turn a somersault at every passing wave.

The old ceremony of introducing to Father Neptune those crossing the line for the first time was not forgotten. In preparation for the visit, a tarpaulin tank was rigged up on the well deck and filled with sea-water. The ancient rites could not be faithfully observed with such a large number of eligibles, and the business soon degenerated into an indiscriminate "ducking" of all on board, regardless of rank. Search parties hauled out those who had not sufficient interest in the proceedings to be present.

We next touched at St. Vincent in the Cape Verde Islands, to replenish coal supplies. The island was the bleakest place seen during the voyage, and to all appearances was absolutely devoid of vegetation. It was inhabited, however, for the usual souvenir-sellers soon surrounded the boat.

Over a dozen enemy craft, ranging in size from 2,000 to 8,000 tons, lay in the harbour. Some of them were new and all quite serviceable vessels, having probably been used in Germany's West African coastal trade. They had evidently been captured early in the war by the Portuguese.

Here we left the rest of the fleet, and made for Madeira, which we reached in a few days. In vivid contrast to the barren rock of St. Vincent, Madeira was clothed in most luxuruant verdure right down to the water's edge.

From the town the land sloped back to the high range in the rear in a succession of garden-terraces. To us, eye-weary for so long with the monochrome of the wintry sea, the view was truly entrancing. We received a hearty welcome from the townspeople who visited the boat, and once more the boat-merchants made hay. Their wares were more varied here, and their prices more European. Canaries were offered at a very low figure, and were bought for relatives in England by many. Wine was also passed up—surreptitiously, of course—and although in France, as we have since learnt, people gaze on the wine when it is all colours of the rainbow, it is safe to say that they have nothing to come up to the standard of the " Madeira " that is sold to travellers on the high seas by the denizens of Funchal. It was said by some who ought to know that there was a spell of " D. T.'s " in every spoonful. One genius who failed to get value for his money conceived the brilliant idea of passing the tops of sheets of Y.M.C.A. paper as banknotes of small denomination. The plan worked well, but the issue was suppressed by Headquarters because one of the officers questioned the purchasing value of one of these notes which was handed back to him as change.

All who were on board the " Demosthenes " must remember the welcome swim off the boat at Madeira. At Cape Town we had been entertained by the natives swimming, diving, and " scrapping " in and under the water, fighting for the meat or coins thrown overboard to them. If silver ran short, coppers wrapped in tin-foil served the purpose. The natives at Madeira went through similar antics, diving off their small craft and invariably upsetting them as they did so. One of our own men essayed a great dive right under the " Demosthenes," and that day too we were treated to the curious spectacle of a soldier in Nature's garb under arrest. The R.S.M. had him " in tow."

After leaving the Cape we had often to answer the alarm, one long blast on the whistle, and scramble up on deck opposite the boats we were to occupy in case of accident to the ship. The ship's captain complimented the C.O., Lieut.-Colonel F. J. Board, on the discipline and speed exhibited by the battalion in carrying out these necessary practices.

We realised, on getting nearer to the scene of the " Big Row," that a close look-out must be kept for hostile submarines. So submarine guards or look-outs were doubled, and all suspicious craft, including whales and porpoises, received close scrutiny until they were seen to be friendly. To train men in anti-U. Boat fire, dry-goods cases were tossed overboard from the stern for targets, and prizes given by the Company-commanders for the best shots. Competition was keen, the novelty of the practice attracting nearly all the best shots of the battalion. Fortunately for them, no hostile submarines put in an appearance, the presence of several vessels of Britain's " Cat Fleet," and a large dirigible balloon, probably keeping them from venturing too far into the Channel.

The Lizard was the first part of England sighted and we kept close along the coast till, in the afternoon of July the 20th, Devonport was reached. It was the middle of summer, the Channel calm as a pond, and dotted with hundreds of small fishing-smacks, with their brown sails hanging limp in the dead calm. On our left, a couple of miles away, the cliffs of old England, clothed in the brilliant green of crops and grass to their very edges, with here and there flocks of sheep and cattle, and above all the rich blue of the summer sky, flecked with small snow-white clouds, made a picture never to be forgotten. Most of us belonged to the second or third generation of Australians, but no Englishman could feel more greatly thrilled with pride of country than we who saw that grand old country for the first time, nor feel greater pride in belonging to the race which had produced so many illustrious men, compatriots of our forbears, who made our Empire the greatest on earth, some of whom, we knew, had sailed in little cockle-shells, from that very port of Plymouth, to win fresh glories for their beloved England.

Truly an empire worth fighting for, an empire of great men, of great deeds worthy of emulation to our utmost endeavour. There were one or two things that greatly impressed us as we drew near to the Old Country. For most of us it was the first time that we had seen an airship or even an aeroplane. The seaplane that flew high over the ship as we entered Devonport was a source of great wonder and admiration. Another incident that gave rise to much excitement and argument was the lightning approach of the destroyer which came out to meet us in the Channel as an escort. Many thought at first that it might be a hostile ship. The marvellous rapidity of its course evoked great astonishment.

Without regret we said " good-bye " to the old " Demosthenes " and by 6 p.m. had began our journey to Salisbury Plain. We arrived at Amesbury, the railway station nearest to our camp, at 3.30 a.m. next morning. Patriotic ladies at Exeter, presided over by the Mayoress, made our long train-trip more endurable by supplying us with hot drinks and other refreshments. This was the first of many evidences shown by the people of England that they were " only too pleased "—as they put it—to do all in their power to make the " Overseas Troops " comfortable during their stay in England. Amesbury is three and a-half miles distant from Lark Hill Camp, but though in our ignorance we carried then loads of no mean weight, the battalion sang all the way to the camp.

It is impossible not to feel in the best of spirits in the early dawn of an English summer day. The air is fragrant with the scent of myriads of wild flowers, which carpet the fields in a blaze of colour and dispute with the crops the possession of the cultivated land, and from the hedgerows and the sky above songbirds sing along one's path. Our appreciation of these things was all the keener after the briny astmosphere we had known for nine long weeks.

At Lark Hill Camp, we were quartered in the usual galvanised iron huts, two of them holding a platoon of men. The camp had all the conveniences of the modern hutment camp, including electric light, baths, washroom, drying room, large and well-equipped kitchens, canteen, and mess-huts. In the vicinity were Y.M.C.A. recreation and reading and writing huts, several cinema halls, and shops in which small necessaries could be bought.

Our stay in Lark Hill was of longer duration than had been anticipated, so that, when our Division left for the front, it was considered the best-trained Overseas Division leaving England for France. Our training, which was very thorough, was carried out according to a syllabus issued by Divisional Headquarters, the whole of the Third Division being then encamped on Salisbury Plain.

Headquarters of our Brigade were under command of Brigadier-General Rankin until Brigadier-General J. H. Cannan came back from the Somme and took over on September 4th.

Parade-hours were longer than those to which we had formerly been accustomed, but the great length of the summer day was fair compensation, so that, after a strenuous day's work, we were able to visit, during daylight hours, the places of interest that abounded in the district. All will remember Stonehenge, the old " Spreading Chestnut Tree," and the ancient buildings in the various villages.

Training consisted of bayonet-fighting, trench-digging, specialist-training, and musketry-practices, these last with a view to increased efficiency in rapid fire (for which our rifle is better adapted than that of the enemy) the importance of which, considering the preponderance of enemy machine-guns over ours, was becoming more and more apparent to the authorities, as the open warfare progressed in France. Features of the musketry-practice were, the firing from trenches on figure-targets, snap-shooting at disappearing targets, and firing with gas-masks on.

Our first idea of trench conditions was obtained at Bustard Trenches, where the Brigade put in a week.

Everyone will remember this initiation into trench life and the exploding of the great mine for experimental purposes. Some may also still smile at the recollection of an officer of the Imperial Army instructing " diggers " from Mount Morgan and other mining centres in the art of handling pick and shovel, showing men how to "take up pick and put down shovel" in the correct military fashion, that is to say "by numbers" or practically so.

Training at Lark Hill also included many route-marches. The great march of the whole Third Division was a rather special event, the vanguard of the Ninth Brigade reaching "Home" before the last of the Eleventh Brigade had started out.

Two periods of leave were granted, to enable us to visit London and distant parts of the British Isles, and a liberal percentage of personnel was allowed leave each week-end.

Towards the end of September the drought, which had raged in the South of England for almost three months, broke in a series of drizzling showers, and beautiful Salisbury Plain degenerated into a swamp almost comparable with Belgium. Certainly the rats which then made their appearance could not have been surpassed in size by the Belgium variety.

On the 27th September we were honoured by a visit from the King. Rain interfered with the proceedings somewhat, and consequently the troops' spirits were at a very low ebb. Even here the irrepressible "dag" did his little bit to cheer things. We were standing "at ease" and the Colonel gave the cautionary command "Battalion will come to attention." Immediately a high-pitched plaintive wail came from the "dag"—"Battalion will get wet"! This was the signal for comments on all sides and each platoon brightened up as the platoon "hardcase" expressed his views of the stunt.

At the first fall of snow, about the end of October, the first most of us had ever seen, there was considerable excitement, and some took this opportunity of paying off old scores. For though one cannot throw a brick at one's O.C. with impunity, there seems to be an unwritten law with regard to snowballing, so that not even one's great aunt could claim exemption if selected as a target. And everybody knows how a lump of thawing snow, well pressed in the hand, feels when it strikes one on the cheek. The enormous "snow-men" put up at that time lasted for many days, and became quite familiar monuments.

Reinforcements for a battalion in France not being sufficient, the 41st battalion was drawn on in order to complete the number, but our first reinforcement, which came with us from Australia, and, later, a draft from the Cyclists' Corps, and our second reinforcement, brought us up to strength again.

Movement orders were received on the 18th November and by the 25th we were in France in No. 2 Rest Camp at Le Havre, having come *via* Southampton. The crossing to France was not a pleasant "Channel trip." We went by night, of course, in a rather small boat, so that it was a case of "on the stairs we lay in pairs," and very few really slept. Also lumps of cork tied round one's body did not add to one's comfort even if one could lie down. From the wharf at Le Havre to the Rest Camp was a distance of six or seven miles, and as we were carrying all our military and worldly belongings, and it was raining hard all the time, with a long hill to be climbed, the march set up a record for weight carried which has never been surpassed. Some weighed their full gear-packs, overcoats, and all, before setting out, and the weights ranged from 100 to 120 lbs.

It was rumoured that the "heads" were eager to get to the line and were impatient at having to spend even a night at Le Havre. However little time was wasted, all hands were roused at 4 a.m. and rushed at a truly desperate pace to the railway station, where, with sweat-sodden garments freezing and trusty packs in the ready position, we waited six seemingly interminable hours for our train. At last to our unspeakable relief, something began to move on the metals, and a long train of cattle-trucks hove alongside, stopping to our disgust, right where we had expected our train to pull up. Some of our number, who had evidently acquired fragments of French at some time in their careers, explained that each "carriage" was intended to carry 40 men or 8 horses. They were right. We were bundled in and the horse boxes got going —average speed three miles per hour. Many, thankful to have their packs carried cheerfully walked much of the way, very occasionally jumping on at a down grade. Sleep was impossible. The route was through Rouen, Abbeville, Boulogne, Calais, Hazebrouck, and finally Bailleul was reached. It was dark after leaving Calais, and soon after passing Hazebrouck we saw for the first time the Verey Lights which illuminate "No Man's Land" throughout the night. There was reason to be thankful that billets were only one and a-half mile from the station, and we quickly sought our beds on reaching our quarters. The following morning, after a "bully and biscuit" breakfast washed down with hot tea, a shift was made to farmhouses further away from Bailleul. There the battalion stayed a week, seven hours each day being devoted to "physical jerks" and bayonet-fighting. Once settled, our spirits rose again as "tucker" improved in quality and quantity. Besides, it was found that by sleeping under four blankets one could be much warmer at night, and those who had not already begun the practice lost no time in taking a mate "for better or worse," and giving him a tryout. Straw was used to ensure greater comfort.

The camp was visited by chocolate-sellers, mostly women and girls, who tramp from all the large towns to distant camps. Needless to say they drove a brisk trade, chocolate and cake being a real food, while bully and biscuits are said to be only mildly nutritious. England was once dubbed "a nation of shopkeepers." In comparison France can hold her own. While the soldier in France continues to draw pay, there will always be some "civvy" glad to swap something with him for it—at a profit.

Spells in the routine of drill we devoted to donning new gas-masks, issued in lieu of the old type. This new type survived the remainder of the war, and is known under various names. In the schedule it appears as "Respirator, Box, Small." To the "digger" it is known as "A Gadget," "Boxpirator," "Gaspirator," "Comme Ca," and "Odag."

One night we were awakened and ordered to put on gas-masks "quick and lively." A long drawn-out hoot that broke the silence of the night caused the alarm. Later it was discovered that it came from a railway engine giving vent to its feelings. It "put the wind up" a good many, especially those who had not yet taken the precaution of keeping their respirators handy before turning in. Someone met an officer that night looking rather worried and asked him if the alarm was dinkum. "Dinkum"? he cried, "My oath, yes! Why the gas came round the corner and gripped me right in the throat"!

The next move was to Armentieres. On the way we became more and more convinced that "a war was on." Passing a wrecked enemy plane, we went on through long strips of wire-entanglement, ruined farms, and the village of Nieppe, which was then pretty badly battered by enemy artillery, the church, as usual, having received most attention. We were billeted in various large buildings in Armentieres, principally colleges, and with that casual manner of appropriating or borrowing things likely to make for greater comfort, which has proved particularly annoying to the guards of many a ration and supply dump belonging to the Imperial Forces, members of the battalion proceeded to "dig in," and coal-fires were soon blazing cheerily in the somewhat airy rooms we occupied.

Thus we arrived at last at the "Big Row," and though the situation was quiet, owing to time of year, an occasional boom from one of our batteries kept us well aware of the fact that the days of preparation belonged to the past and the real thing lay ahead.

"Plank Avenue" — Armentieres.

PHASE II.

CHAPTER 1.

Billeted in Armentieres.—The First Shells.—Christmas Eve.—Off to the Trenches.—Trench Life.—Spies, Rats, and Anecdotes.

Armentieres. In that name—pronounced, of course, "Amen-tears," by all of us—there lies a host of memories. It was there that most of us first experienced the sensations of being shelled, there that our battalion received its baptism of fire.

The previous chapter has described our arrival in the old Flemish city, once the centre of great textile industry, now a heap of ruins. In December, 1916, the town had not suffered greatly from shell-fire; there was a fair percentage of the population still living there, and many shops were doing a brisk trade among the troops, especially in the way of souvenirs, laces, silks, postcards, and the like. And so, what with pleasurable evenings spent at the numerous estaminets and "Eat-up Joints," and the joys of a cinema show at the Y.M.C.A. hall, Armentieres became almost home-like, despite the frost and snow, and the popular chorus "I want to go home."

The week prior to our first period in the trenches many wild rumours were current, most of them in connection with the peace terms set out by Germany, those first outrageous terms. Some went so far as to think that peace would be actually signed before we reached the line. One rumour, which gained a great deal of credence, was that the Kaiser had asked for thirty days' armistice to withdraw his troops from Belgium and France. Another story that went the rounds was that Sir Douglas Haig had been killed near the front; and so on *ad inf.*

It is believed to be a fact that the Saxon troops opposing us at Armentieres raised a board on their parapet, or on our wire, bidding us shoot high as peace was very near now.

Life in Armentieres had sufficient variety to make the time pass quickly. The main part of the day would be spent in training. Lewis Gunners were given lectures and practised in the Hospice Civile. The scouts made nightly trips to the trenches, and had their first glimpse of "No Man's Land," and everyone was made conversant with the new box-respirator, and impressed with the danger of gas and the supreme importance of being able to manipulate the mask as quickly as possible.

On Christmas Eve, the Third Divisional Pierrots, better known as the "Coo-ees," gave their first show at the Cinema Hall, a building that formed part of a large Ecole

Professionale. Everyone knows the "Coo-ees," but they had not then yet won their reputation for being one of the best shows in France. Some of the original performers stayed in the company right through until the Australians left France. Considering the excellence of the entertainment put up on that first Christmas Eve, to say that they improved out of all recognition as time went on is to pay them the highest possible compliment.

When one thinks of those days at Armentieres, all those civilians "carrying on" but a few hundred yards from the front line, the big-gun emplacements concealed throughout the city, the ever-menacing danger of a bombardment, which only a supposed mutual understanding temporarily held off—for our artillery in like manner had Lille at its mercy—and when one thinks of what happened later on and considers the fate of many towns and villages on the Somme which were even further from the German guns, and the ultimate destruction of Armentieres itself, the amazing sense of security that pervaded the place absolutely passes all comprehension. It was as if a man walked on the edge of a volcano. There is no doubt that many of the people stayed on to the bitter end, taking risks daily, just with a view to making as much money as they could. The estaminet keepers made small fortunes, even though champagne could be purchased then for five francs a bottle, and despite the occasion when Madame and her satellites, in their eagerness to see a Boche 'plane being driven down, would rush from the café, leaving their bottles of "Rouge et Blanc" to the tender mercies of the blasé but unscrupulous "digger." The hail of "mustard shells" that Fritz finally sent over drove the last of these "die-hards" from the old town.

Billets were good. The battalion occupied large substantial buildings, schools, and factories, which were very numerous in Armentieres. There were extensive cellars to flee to in case of bombardment, in fact they were used more than once when retaliation was feared after a more than usually big "strafe" by our artillery. The companies that camped in the Hospice Civile will remember being rudely awakened one night, and ordered into the cellars, long after the strafiing had ceased. Very reluctantly gathering up blankets and gear, all descended into the depths, and having wedged themselves in somehow in those narrow vaults, rolled themselves up warmly for a good sleep. But an order came along to return *toute de suite* to the upper regions, and the subsequent comments of the long-suffering troops will not bear repeating.

Occasionally, too, there were false alarms of gas. When the "wind dangerous" notice was up, everyone had to go about with his respirator at the "alert." One Scotchman of Headquarters fame, during one of these night alarms, struggled with his mask for about ten minutes, but failing to adjust it properly, threw it away in disgust, saying " that he would rather be gassed than suffocate in a —————— thing like that." Of course, no one was really accustomed to the masks in those days.

The first time, perhaps, that we realised our proximity to Fritz was one quiet Sunday afternoon, when three shells went shrieking overhead and crashed near the cathedral, killing a sergeant of the 42nd Battalion. They " put the wind up " us with a vengeance. Someone said afterwards that our artillery had fired shots into Lille, trying a new gun.

The cathedral was partly destroyed before the battalion arrived in Armentieres, and the church of St. Roch, situated in a part of the town nearest the line, was a complete ruin. Most of the large buildings were scarred and chipped in some way or other, but one or two seemed to have escaped all damage, notably the Blue Blind Factory near the Pont de Nieppe road, and a domed bank building in the main street between " Half-past Eleven Square " and the station. It was, therefore, rumoured, of course, that these must be German-owned concerns. It is worthy of note here that the Place de l'Hotel de Ville, rechristened " Half-past Eleven Square " by the British (that being the time when the Town Hall clock stopped on being hit) was never called anything else from that day, even by the French themselves.

Three days before Christmas, the whole battalion marched to Steenwerck, some five or six miles, to be reviewed for the first time by Sir Douglas Haig. The day was far from enjoyable, as one had to stand about in the mud for hours, and, naturally, it rained.

A history of this kind would not be complete without some reference to the hot baths supplied to the troops in an old brewery alongside the Lys Canal, just off the Nieppe road. These baths are unique in the experience of the 41st Battalion. No trickling shower-bath there, but complete immersion in enormous brewing vats, which would hold as many as ten at a time. They were indeed " some " baths.

Probably we all looked forward to our first " trip " to the trenches. It may seem an amazing idea to us now that we really know the horrors of war ; but we were then new to the game and were longing to prove ourselves as good as the other divisions, which had already taken part in all sorts of marvellous stunts. But undoubtedly the chief cause of our impatience was curiosity.

Our turn came on Christmas Eve of all days, when we relieved the 35th Battalion. The specialists had preceded the remainder of the battalion the day before, and by noon on the 24th the relief was complete. Nearly every member of the battalion had visited some part of this sector before, as, apart from reconnaissances by officers, N.C.O.'s and scouts, there had been working-parties. Many will remember the humorous side of digging trenches to bury cables, as well as the discomforts and inevitable "windiness," how the "prone" had to be assumed more rapidly than most were used to, when "Parapet Joe" started sweeping the landscape. Perhaps some can still recall the "Tommy" officer urging the men to dig deeper, though the mud and water were well nigh knee-deep, and how the exhausted "diggers," taking advantage of the darkness, kept imitating the ultra-cultured intonation peculiar to the British officer.

Armentieres, one might say, occupied a position actually in the line; that is to say, it was only a matter of a few hundred yards from estaminet to front-line trench, while the suburb of La Chapelle d'Armentieres extended out still further, and was in a ruinous state, owing to the presence of our artillery there. That first duckboard trail in to the line is memorable not only because of its novelty, but also for the fact that the troops carried full packs, blankets-up, and all, a really prodigious weight including 170 rounds of ammunition. There was many a slip on faulty duckboards and one often found oneself tightly wedged between the narrow trench walls.

Before entering the long communication trench just across the railway line, the track led past a large semi-ruined asylum, part of which then served as a gum-boot store.

These high rubber boots were splendid as a protection against water but could not keep out the cold, and the severe weather of that record winter, 1916-1917, set in shortly after the battalion's debut in the trenches. Even in December, to men fresh from Australia, the cold seemed sufficiently intense, but it was nothing to what we were to experience in mid-January and February. The communication trench leading to our sector passed near an old brickwork, and hence the name "Brickstack Lane," Battalion Headquarters were at "Square Farm," north-east of La Chapelle d'Armentieres. Across the road from which was Fochabers Dump. It was here that one poor man, "losing touch" one night in the dark, got so inextricably tangled up in barbed wire that he had to remain there till wire cutters were found—by no means a pleasant adventure. A rather risky "overland route," with a narrow-guage line for bringing up rations on a truck, led from the dump to the subsidiary line, but the communication trench was generally adhered to, as stray shots were frequently flying around.

In those days of eternal trench-warfare it will be remembered that there was a regular system, consisting of front line with fire-bays and high breastworks, support-line about two hundred yards in rear, and further back the subsidiary lines or "Subsids" as they were generally called. Each trench had its name, and some bore most incongruous titles, such as "Piccadilly," "Strand," and so forth. The three communication trenches, forward in the battalion sector, were called "Lothian Avenue," "Central Avenue," and "Forte Egale." The front-line sector, some fifteen hundred yards wide, consisted of a series of bays and fairly large gaps, which had to be patrolled at night. Between companies there were considerable strips of "No Man's Land." All four companies were allotted a section of front line, the battalion flanks being protected by small detached garrisons or bombing posts, and also by patrols at night. "Fritz" was only eighty yards from our line as the "Mushroom Salient," which was manned at night by two small detached parties, generally termed "listening posts." But the width of "No Man's Land" varied, being as great as three hundred and twenty yards opposite what was known as "No. 1 locality." At that time the battalion was almost at full strength, and one platoon per company, or sometimes two, were sufficient to man the fire bays, leaving one platoon for the supports and two in the subsidiaries. Between the latter and the supports was an intermediate trench, known as "Headquarters Walk," where the bombers made their home. The dug-outs, especially in the supports were—well, in fact, they were not dug-outs at all, but still it is marvellous what security one felt when crouched under a thin sheet of iron, whilst a few assorted bits of ironmongery were whizzing over in search of the Stokes Battery. Those noisy Stokes behind the supports annoyed Fritz not a little. It sometimes happened that after a heavy fall of snow the iron roof of one of these dug-outs would give way. One day a cookhouse collapsed in this manner and fell across the support trench, blocking the track. Someone near the spot at the time hurried to the cook's rescue, but after clearing away the debris, all he could see was a conglomeration of dixies, pots, and pans. The cook was "napoo."

There was a signaller at headquarters who invented a fine decorative scheme for the embellishment of the vicinity of his dug-out. He used to collect "duds" and stick them in rows along the top of the trench like a rampart. If he heard a shell lob anywhere near without exploding he would run to the spot where it fell, and triumphantly bring it back, still hot from its flight, to swell his museum. Had "Fritz" been able to get a direct hit with an "H. E." on this corner of our trench-system, there would have been "something doing."

It is now well known that Fritz was kept well informed by spies of nearly all our movements in and about Armentieres, and this will explain the "strafe" he put up on the battalion on that Christmas Eve, as we took over. Till then "mumps" had been our worst enemy and caused a good many casualties, but now we had started on the "dinkum" thing, and sad to relate, just a few of the 41st who marched out from billets that night, never saw the light of Christmas Day. Our casualties were four killed and three wounded. Not only from spies in the town was Fritz able to glean his information. There was just a possibility that one of his men, dressed in our uniform, could cross over at night under cover of the railway embankment, wander through our lines, and escape without being challenged, as in those days the platoons were so strong numerically that one man more or less was seldom noticed. There was one case of a wandering South African (?) who could not give a satisfactory account of himself, and was supposed to have escaped from custody afterwards.

The spy scare was very prevalent at this time. Once near the old Asylum an Australian official photographer was challenged and held up. And then, invariably, all Pioneer officers would be halted in the front line and examined with great suspicion. The officer, too, who questioned the South African " Bird " in his dug-out, is said to have done some marvellous prestidigitation with his revolver, which must have given his prisoner some very anxious moments. It was, in fact, this general " windiness " that gave rise to the tales that there were Hun snipers all over the country, far behind our front line. These " snipers " were our own men, firing their rifles anywhere and at any time, evidently to give themselves greater confidence. Very careful were we then not to make too much noise on the way into the trenches. Even as far back as the Asylum, all talking and smoking was forbidden, as if Fritz were quite near, and rifles had to be carried at the trail.

CHRISTMAS, 1916.

Boxes of Comforts were distributed among the men in the trenches, but it was a cold, cheerless day, and there were the usual artillery " strafes." At Christmas-time at night we could plainly hear Fritz celebrating the festival, singing songs to accordion accompaniment, and laughing and joking. In case this music would charm some of us across No Man's Land, an order was issued, forbidding fraternisation. Trench life is monotonous. The stew brought up in dixies at night was one of the bright spots in one's existence. A man would have twenty-four hours in the front line and then go back to the supports for the same period, and then to the subsidiaries, and so back to the firing line once again, a continuous round. Although this sector was notoriously quiet, to the unsophisticated it seemed at times anything but tranquil. Merely to raise a periscope slightly over the top of the sandbags of the parapet, meant probably a veritable hail of " Whiz-bangs," concentrated towards that spot. During the day the Hun snipers would be very active and a man took a fair risk in exposing his head too long above the breastworks. Rarely indeed did one catch sight of the enemy, unless out on patrol with the scouts. When our artillery had a " mad minute " or two, concentrating on Fritz's front line, it afforded quite a spectacle for our men. Mud, sandbags, and duckboards would fly pell-mell into the air, causing exclamations of delight from all sides, except from Fritz himself, who was safely in a dug-out or in his supports at those lively periods. British gunners were behind us until the 3rd Divisional Artillery took over. One great feature of the nights was Fritz's searchlight, which swept over " No Man's Land," and though many tried, no one succeeded in extinguishing those dazzling rays. His Verey lights, too, were a source of wonder for a while, and it was rumoured that a fair sum was on offer to anyone who could " souvenir " a pistol from which these lights were fired. And who does not remember listening to the seemingly slow passage overhead of " Lazy Lizz's " offspring—our " Lazy Lizz " of Steenwerck ? Being new to this sort of life, many took a keen delight in taking pot shots across " No Man's Land " at nothing in particular, just to let off their feelings, as it were. But apart from that, the intense cold made frequent movement of the bolt absolutely necessary. Of course, if a hostile plane appeared overhead, there was a regular bombardment from rifles and Lewis Guns. But planes were not very frequent over the trenches in those early days. The nights seemed abnormally long and as the eye grew weary with the strain of watching, the wiring-posts and stumps assumed larger proportions, and stranger shapes, and seemed actually to move nearer, and one's heart beat faster, and one's grip on the rifle grew firmer as one waited expectantly for an attack that never came. The writer vividly remembers the sentinel in one bay turning to him and saying in a horrible whisper " I saw a hand raised just out there in front of our wire, look out for a bomb," but lo ! it was only a large rat that jumped across some heaped debris beyond the parapet. Yes, rats were a predominating factor in our life. They were almost as plentiful as the smaller creature which irritated us all so fearfully later on when the winter had passed. Rats not only devoured the " tucker," but gnawed the equipment, but for all that, one felt friendly towards them in comparison with the Boche across the way. It used to be great sport in enticing rats with a piece of cheese stuck on the end of your fixed bayonet, and then pulling the trigger. Talking of rats, one cannot but recall a rather amusing little incident that occurred one night. A well-known officer, one whom the Americans would call a " gun man," was patrolling the trenches on his own, sneaking silently along the duckboards in a stooping attitude, with his revolver ready cocked in his hand, when suddenly on turning a corner he saw a dark shape moving above the parapet silhouetted against the moonlight. In accents tense with horror he challenged the shape, pointing his revolver at the same time. Then the moon shone out clearly and revealed his prisoner, who did not linger over the " kamerad " act, but scampered away " quick and lively " to his funk-hole.

History does not relate what remarks the officer made when he realised his unnecessary show of heroism. All kinds of strange shapes this officer is said to have challenged at the point of his pistol, such as kerosene tins, and "duds" lying about the parapets and parados. In consequence of this stealthy creeping through the trenches at night, pistol foremost, many extraordinary things happened, which cannot but strike one as ridiculous. A man was once coming along the trench towards him and slipped off the duckboards. The noise he made so startled our "pistol" friend that he also lost his balance, slipped up and landed on his back, probably expecting a Hun to pounce on him any moment. Another time he came to the corner of a fire-bay, where a sentry was standing, nearly asleep. All the sentry could see, as he half opened his eyes, was a revolver with a hand on the end of it protruding round the bend. Immediately he came "on guard," and with a yell struck at the apparition with his bayonet. Later there had to be explanations, but it is difficult to say which of them had the "wind up" most.

Those night patrols by each platoon, they seem trivial now, but were then filled with exciting and breathless moments—two men with fixed bayonets stealthily filing through the muddy trench to bridge the gap between the two companies, the halt at the meeting point to move a board or piece of sandbag to a prearranged position, to let the patrol from the other company know that your patrol had come and gone.

The scouts, under Lieutenant Douglas, did some great work during those first weeks of trench warfare. Every night found them increasing in daring, so that before long the battalion might find itself master of "No Man's Land," for Fritz had that reputation, indisputably, when we commenced operations in that sector. Trench repair-work and wiring were carried out at night, but the bright moonlight at the beginning of January made the latter work very risky, and unfortunately there were casualties. The intense frost made the part played by the covering party to the wirers painfully arduous, as a man had to lie out in a shell hole on the alert for an hour or more, until, numbed and stiff with the cold, he often found himself unable to move, and had to be helped, or even carried, back to the trench.

Among the many characters that held the Armentieres front about this time was one "Alice," belonging to another battalion—lover of all things beautiful. Asked, the first night in, why he persisted in exposing himself, he answered "I like to watch these here Various Lights." "Alice" did his bit. He acted as a warning to the carelessly curious, being "souvenired" by Fritz while mooning round "No Man's Land." "Oh Alice! where art thou"? After a week or ten days in the line the battalion would be relieved, generally by the 43rd, and march back to billets in

"Kamerad."

Armentieres, to resume a semi-civilised estaminet life, intermingled with night working-parties in the trenches under the 11th Field Engineers, which usually meant getting up at two o'clock. And then, after a few days' "rest," back to the trenches again.

CHAPTER 2.

The Raids.—The Diggers' Philosophy.—Le Bizet and Le Touguet.—Types of Shells.—Ploegsteert.—Catacombs.—March to Bayinghem.

During the winter months, when fighting along the whole front was practically stationary, the only infantry action which took place was in the form of raids on the enemy trench-systems, the object being to take prisoners, or find out by other means what regiments were opposing us, what their intentions might be, and anything that would be of general interest for the Allied cause, besides disorganising the enemy locally, and showing him that we were not hibernating, but on the contrary were very much alive and active. For this purpose a raiding party was formed some weeks before the battalion went into the line, and an officer and some eighty other ranks went through a course of instruction at a raiding school. The Officer in charge was Lieutenant Asche. The first raid took place in the early morning of 31st January, 1917. A fighting patrol of two officers and eighteen men left our trenches at 4 a.m. in an endeavour to attack an enemy listening-post, which had been located by our scouts in front of the Boche wire opposite to No. 1 locality. Owing to the snow on the ground all the raiders were camouflaged in white overalls. Briefly this is what occurred. When the patrol got to within fifty yards of the enemy wire, they were detected and attacked by machine-gun fire, bombs, and trench mortars, assisted by Fritz's search-lights. They withdrew hurriedly towards our wire under heavy fire from the enemy front line. Some of the party missed the gaps in our wire, and had to be guided in by our scouts, who went out to meet them. Meanwhile the two officers were hit, Lieutenant Findlay was severely wounded and later returned to Australia, being unfit for further service. Lieutenant Asche fell with a bullet in his chest, having made the supreme sacrifice. Thus the battalion lost one of its finest officers. He was a fearless and resolute leader, respected and admired by everyone who knew him. It seems that the white overalls did not prove satisfactory, especially when the men were moving among the stumps and posts in "No Man's Land." Also our patrol greatly under-estimated the enemy's vigilance, for the men did not crawl over "No Man's Land," but simply walked across in a stooping posture, so that Fritz, immediately he detected their movements, waited and allowed them to come quite close up before opening fire. At the time this happened the Boche front line was fairly heavily manned opposite the point where our patrol was operating. All our dead and wounded were brought back to our lines. A few days later, at the beginning of February, another raiding party was formed, consisting of three officers and forty-three men, who were sent to a Brigade School for training. Scouting parties from these raiders used to operate nightly over the sector on which they were intending to carry out the next raid. On the 11th of February the opportunity came. Taking advantage of a bombardment and raid that same night by the 10th Brigade on the right flank, our raiders made an attack on the enemy's trenches. Previous artillery action, mainly trench-mortars, had partly cut the wire at the place selected, and the party had planned to enter the enemy's front trench under cover of artillery barrage and trench-mortars, with machine-guns covering his machine-gun emplacements and communication trenches. At 7.50 p.m. over the top once more went the raiders, each man knowing well his allotted task and ready to carry it out to the best of his power. They lay up under cover in shell-holes, while the enemy's wire was submitted to a one-minute bombardment. The barrage was then lengthened, and played for three minutes on Fritz's front line. Immediately it lifted again on to his supports our men leaped up, and advanced towards the spot where the gap in the enemy's wire was supposed to be. But their luck was out. The wire was not sufficiently cut, and when they endeavoured to pass through it in small parties a hail of shrapnel and "Minnies" descended upon them, naturally causing great confusion. As quickly as possible our men withdrew, and took what cover they could find in shell-holes and the like, and recognising the failure of the attempt small parties at a time were detached to regain our lines. While they were withdrawing, Fritz's searchlights swept the whole of "No Man's Land," materially assisting his machine-gun fire. Most of our casualties occurred at the enemy's wire, and while the men were getting back to shell-holes for cover. Communication, too, was delayed owing to the telephone wires being cut, both in "No Man's Land" and behind our parapet, so that information had to be sent back by runner to the nearest Company Headquarters, which was "A" Company, and thence through to Battalion Headquarters. As soon as it was known that the raid had failed, and the party was returning, the artillery fire was discontinued, and shortly afterwards Fritz's strafe also ceased. Lieutenant Douglas, the scout officer, was badly wounded in this raid, which proved to be the last encounter he took part in, for he never rejoined the battalion. In all, two men were killed and eight wounded, the wounds being caused chiefly by shrapnel and H.E. fragments. Private W. S. Weeks who carried Lieutenant Douglas back to our lines under heavy fire was awarded the D.C.M. This brave lad, who later rose to the rank of Sergeant, "carried on" until August 28th, 1918, when near the famous Fargny Mill he fell in action.

The trench-mortars during the first few weeks in the Armentieres Sector were full of surprises—sometimes it would be our wire that the "plum puddings" would play havoc with, at other times a section of carefully sandbagged parapet in our front line would be rudely knocked about and lacerated. The bombers, too, had their wild moments. Once they shot up a Boche cookhouse with rifle grenades, and thus brought on a ding-dong fight. The platoons in the front line would have to bear the brunt of any return hate that might come along, as the bombers, after firing a few rounds of grenades, used to "get," at the "toute."

A few days after the second raid described above, while the battalion was out for a spell, another raiding party was formed and sent to a school to practise for a small attack on Fritz's trenches, and patrol parties did reconnaissance work each night during the week. While on patrol on the night of February 18th, Lieutenant J. Epps, one of our most popular officers, was killed by a bullet from a machine-gun. Lieutenant Epps had been bombing officer and also O.C., Headquarters Details in Armentieres. He was another great loss to the battalion. Many will remember how wild he would get if he thought that any of his "birds" in the bombing platoon were being sent out on too many risky enterprises, such as wiring by moonlight. He knew how to look after his men.

Three or four days before the actual raid, preparations were in active progress. The battalion relieved the 43rd on the 21st. This time the famous "Mushroom" salient was abandoned except for one Lewis gun on each flank. Also one company was kept in reserve in the subsidiary trench, of which one platoon held the main line behind the salient at night.

On the night of the 21st a small party of Huns attempted to effect an entrance into our front trench at this salient, but they were spotted by a Lewis gun crew, who fired on them, wounding one. The hostile party retired, leaving a pistol, bayonet, cap with badges, and a pair of gloves on our wire.

The reserve company was busy wiring across the "Mushroom" the following night, also behind the gaps, and on the 23rd our artillery bombarded the enemy's trenches and wire defences with a view to the raid shortly to come off. This was repeated on the next night, Fritz replying with "Shrap" and "Minnies," using search-lights and Verey lights very freely.

The 26th was the date finally arranged for the raid, and the night before was spent in laying telephone wires and constructing bridges across ditches. Also a small dressing station was fixed up in the support line, south of Lothian Avenue.

February 26th. Final arrangements were now complete for the raid. The raiders came straight from the Brigade School, and were fully equipped at Battalion Headquarters with bridging-ladders and traverser-mats. The party numbered about fifty, including three officers. All crossed our parapet safely and reached the point of assembly in " No Man's Land " at 12.25 a.m. on the morning of the 27th. The scouts had been out previously to inspect the enemy's wire and reported that a fair gap had been made by our artillery. But it proved afterwards that this was not the case and hence the failure of this raid. At 12.30 a.m. our artillery commenced a barrage on the enemy's trenches, our men now being close up to his wire ; when this had ceased the officers in charge of the raiders examined the wire for a distance of a hundred yards and more along the front, but found no gap, and estimated that even at its narrowest part it would take at least a quarter of an hour to cut only a small gap by hand. A general withdrawal was then ordered, the party fortunately regaining our front line without any casualties. The enemy used two searchlights, but these were rendered practically useless by our smoke bombs, fired from Stokes Mortars, which very effectually clouded the lights. The excellence of the artillery barrage gave the men increased confidence, and although the raid failed to accomplish its object, the smooth working of all the details augured well for future attempts. The telephone-system worked well, the three alternative lines remaining intact throughout, allowing information to be transmitted promptly from the front parapet back to Brigade Headquarters. The artillery retaliation of the enemy caused a few casualties in our front line. Scout Bob Perkins made a name for himself, as he was the only one who had energy enough to " hump " a great ditching-bridge back with him from " No Man's Land." In this raid our men wore body armour for the first and last time.

On this sector the battalion was singularly unfortunate in all raids undertaken. The failure on every occasion to penetrate the enemy's wire exposed our raiders to heavy fire and forced a speedy retirement. Raids carried out from time to time on our flanks met with varying success. At 11·30 p.m. on the same night that Lieutenant Douglas was wounded, the Tynesiders went over the top two hundred strong and brought back seventeen prisoners, but their casualties were very heavy.

During all this period the weather was extremely cold. After heavy falls of snow and slight frosts at the beginning of January, the actual freeze-up commenced about the 18th of the month and lasted without a break till 11th February. That phenomenal winter proved terribly trying to the men in the trenches, and it was marvellous how well most of them came through it. "Trench feet" even did not trouble us very much, thanks to careful supervision, but the "Third Division cough" became a byword. The whale-oil issued for rubbing into the feet came in very useful for frying biscuits in. It is strange to think that some saw snow for the first time in their lives that winter, and enjoyed their first sliding on ice which was strong enough to bear a house.

March found the battalion installed once more in billets in Armentieres. Working-parties were provided for repair-work in the trenches, and schools and classes were started for snipers, Lewis gunners, revolver practice, and gas instruction. Increasing respect for gas was noticeable at this time, and any man who was unable to put his gas mask on in six seconds was considered as good as dead!

In connection with the raids, mention must be made of Lance-Corporal Dodds of the scouts, the first man in the battalion to receive the "M.M." Later he became a platoon-sergeant, and fell in action near Passchendaele. Another scout, Private Albert Lambert, also won the "M.M." for conspicuous coolness and bravery under fire during a raid, bringing in the wounded from "No Man's Land."

During the second week in March, we were again holding the line, carrying on the usual routine of passive resistance, patrolling, doing engineering repairs, wiring, and so on. Casualties were few and far between, and were mainly evacuations of sick to hospital.

It was now that the battalion lost a well-known figure, who had made himself popular with all ranks, namely, Major Milne, who was transferred to the command of the 36th Battalion. Major Milne—or "Jock" as he was familiarly known—had made his personality felt in the battalion, and the news of his death in action on the Somme in the spring of 1918 filled all 41st men who had known him with that deep feeling of regret which only personal loss is capable of evoking.

On the 10th of March we were relieved by the 35th Battalion. This continuous round of "in and out" of the trenches has been inimitably pictured by Captain Bairnsfather, and though one may laugh at the humorous aspect of the business portrayed by the artist, one cannot help shuddering at the thought of what the actual thing meant— the dreary, monotonous existence in the frost-bound trenches. The mention of Bairnsfather suggests an analogy between the spirit of his famous cartoons and the irrepressible air of casualness—the "don't-care-a-damn-what-happens" air of the "digger" amid the mire and misery of a Messines or Ypres battlefield. This invaluable gift of being able to adapt oneself to every circumstance and find a humorous element in what would appear, to some minds, to be a hopeless situation, seems to be the birthright of the Britisher, and affords much food for reflection to all foreigners with whom he comes into contact. The French may say that the Englishman is "phlegmatique," but he is infinitely more than that, and this war has brought out his true qualities, penetrating beneath the veneer of his typical cold reserve. The Australian, is, by nature, far less reserved than the Tommy, and so we find in him all the traits of the true Britisher accentuated to the highest degree, giving him an almost exaggerated air of causal coolness and devil-may-care in the face of overwhelming and disastrous circumstances. Ancient history tells of Diogenes, the philosopher in his tub ; his modern counterpart is surely the "Aussie," the philosopher of the shell-hole.

Our long sojourn in the Armentieres sector came to an end at last, and the battalion moved to Le Bizet on March the 14th. On our last day in the line in the old sector Fritz was very active, sending over salvos of H.E. all along the subsidiary line, where two men were buried whilst asleep in their dug-out. He evidently wished to give us a good send-off.

The battalion was a few days in Le Bizet in billets. During this time large engineering parties were supplied for work in the Le Touquet sector by day and night. The rest of the battalion carried on with the usual training. On the 19th we relieved the 43rd at Le Touquet. Our front extended from the river Lys in the South to the Warnave River in the North, a total frontage of 3,000 yards. The Houplines-Warneton railway ran through the centre of this front. The trenches here were very shallow compared to those that we had been used to, and required continual draining. The snipers on both sides put in a good deal of work here, and Fritz put the "wind up" with his Minnenwerfer strafes. One "rum-jar" lobbed on "D" Company's Headquarters, killing one man and shell-shocking the O.C.

For the benefit of a few who may not know, a "rum-jar" was the name we gave to a Minnenwerfer shell of 9·5 calibre. By this time we had learnt a lot about Fritz's "visiting cards." One had no longer to be a military expert to differentiate between a 5.9 and a 4.2, and one soon knew instinctively the approximate distance away one of these was likely to land, thus saving a good deal of unnecessary ducking and mental uneasiness. The "Whizz-Bang" (77 m.m.) never lost its element of startling surprise, and after the lightning passage of the first across the parapet, all heads would be well down under cover. Those shells seemed to shave the very hair off one's head. The larger type of H.E. shell, droning along far overhead, did not worry the front-line man ; he would smile to himself and think how headquarters would get the "wind up," and would be rudely reminded that there was a war on.

Then there were "Pineapples," really very small trench-mortar shells with wind-vanes to steady their flight, which led to a belief at first that they were "aerial torpedoes." "Minnies" varied in size. The large kind was a fearful missile, guaranteed to penetrate any ordinary dug-out. They were said to possess the peculiarity of changing direction in mid-air before they fell "plomp" to the ground. On detecting the faint whistle of one approaching, if one were in a fire-bay, one would just have time to watch it turn on its downward rush and then dive round the corner at the safest end of the bay; but he who hesitated was lost.

While we held the Le Touquet front, the New Zealanders near us were raided three nights in succession, but never allowed Fritz to penetrate their lines, beating him off every time with heavy losses.

There was an unfortunate occurrence on our last day in, one of our 18-pounder shells falling short during a strafe, causing five casualties, some fatal. This is only mentioned to show how seldom an accident of that sort happened in those days.

We left Le Bizet on April the 5th. Ploegsteert Wood or "Plugstreet"—as it is more familiarly called—is memorable to us on account of the "Catacombs" and gas shells rather than for any association with King Albert of Belgium, who, they say used to hunt therein in pre-war days. Here the battalion at first acted as support to the 42nd, occupying huts and farm buildings. The Battalion Headquarters out-building at Creslow Farm, some may remember was partially burned down on the 6th. Engineering parties were daily supplied until the battalion relieved the 42nd in the Ploegsteert-St. Ives sector. This time Fritz made two or three attempts to raid our trenches, but never succeeded. We had Bavarians opposing us now, who were supposed to be some of his best troops, far more warlike, anyhow, than the Saxon crowd who had occupied the Lille front about Christmas.

One night our patrol was crossing a gap when a Boche officer and a few men issued from a dugout and grabbed the last man of the party. Hearing his call the rest turned back, and the Fritzes quickly made off to their own lines, leaving their prisoner. This sort of thing made the patrols very wary, and not a little "windy."

On another occasion two men met at a bend of a trench, which crossed this unguarded gap. Each challenged the other, thinking he was a Fritz, and started firing, one with a revolver and the other with his rifle. That they did not hit each other shows how much they had the "wind up." At last one of them started using some of the more lurid Australian language, and the other recognised a "cobber," but even so, he was in a terrible state of mind, fearing he had shot one of our own men ; in fact, both were relieved to discover that mutual windiness had saved the situation.

While in the Ploegsteert trenches a small silent raid was attempted, but failed in its object. Lieutenant Harvey was killed that night.

On coming out, the battalion marched to the famous catacombs at Hyde Park Corner. They were a series of large dug-outs tunnelled into Hill 63, and contained accommodation for about 2,000 men, with separate detached dug-outs for offices and so forth. The tunnellers had been working here during the winter, some of the 41st being amongst them—men who had joined them soon after our arrival at Bailleul. In addition to the tunnellers, there was a small party of the 41st engaged during these winter months in railway construction work between Dunkerque and Poperinghe. This railway played an important part in the big offensive at Ypres later in the year. Lieutenant Wellings was in charge of this party. Gas was now beginning to play an important part in the fighting. At first it was mainly brought up in cylinders, and directed in clouds against the enemy, whenever the wind was favourable. There was an organised gas-attack of this kind on April the 24th, and, in order to find out what effect our gas had had on the Hun, a patrol under Lieutenant C. H. Butler went out at Anton's Farm about an hour after the attack. But the raiders were observed while trying to cut the wire and had to withdraw.

Apart from that little incident, nothing of importance occurred during the remainder of our stay in this sector, and on being relieved we marched back again to Armentieres, whence two days later the whole battalion set forth on the long trail to Bayinghem. On the first day eighteen miles were covered, Grand-sec-Bois being the scene of the first night's bivouac. Renescure was reached the next day, and the third day's march took us to Wizernes, near St. Omer. Here a swim in the canal and a concert in the evening refreshed everyone physically and mentally. On May the 4th the march was resumed *via* Lumbres to Bayinghem, where billets were found in farm-houses and barns, and back-area training commenced.

The march to Bayinghem was a long and trying one, especially the first day, when the guides missed the way, but it is surprising how quickly a man forgets his weariness, after he has finally flung off his pack, had a good wash, and a hot tea. Then what joy to lie at ease on the straw, rolled up in one's blankets with an issue " fag " between one's lips, and to think, before sleep overtakes one, how fortunate one is not only to be out of Fritz's reach, but to be back again where the gold-flowing bock and dark-eyed desmoiselles soothe the war-weary heart, and to relegate the Hun and all his devilish devices to the realms of oblivion.

PHASE III.

CHAPTER 1.

Bayinghem.—Training and Sports.—Pont de Nieppe.—Working-parties.—Ploegsteert Wood.—In the St. Ives Sector.—Preparation for Messines.—7th June, Battle of Messines.—Hillside Camp.—Anecdotes.—At Blanche Maison.

When we arrived at Bayinghem, France was at her best, with blue unruffled skies, and the landscape a garden of beauty, with trees and flowers in richest verdure. Having experienced the rigours of her winter, one now felt inclined to take a more lenient view of her climatic shortcomings.

In this Eden, the battalion carried out a course of some of the most systematic training it had ever undergone, commencing with specialist training, trench-to-trench and open warfare fighting, culminating in two Brigade schemes, which were held in the presence of General Sir H. Plumer, the Corps, Divisional, and Brigade Commanders, who expressed themselves satisfied with these exercises. When one remembers the wonderful success of the 7th June, the Battle of Messines, this narrative would fall a long way short of its purpose if mention were not made of the amount of staff work and training, even down to minor details, which contributed towards the success of that great battle. All our schemes were carried out over exact replicas of our own and the German trenches, " split-locked " out, on ground similar to the La Douve Valley, and our Brigade stunts were undertaken with all other arms, and were run absolutely to time-table, with nothing omitted except the artillery barrages. Even the carrying-parties, as they will remember to their sorrow, wended their weary way laden with the real articles. One may also remember the replica to scale of our sector of operations, which could be seen at Brune Gaye, and the smaller models prepared by the engineers at Pont de Nieppe.

While at Bayinghem time was found to hold a sports meeting, and there was very keen rivalry between the three hundred or so competitors for the prizes, which amounted to some fifty pounds.

In spite of the hard training, seven hours a day, it was with many regrets that we left this peaceful scene, and turned our faces once more towards the thunder of the guns. On the march back, the men were in great heart, and put up such a good performance, that they raised the battalion from last place in the Brigade's estimation, going down, to the place of honour on the march back. During the last week in May, the battalion entered upon billet life at Pont de Nieppe. At this time, the village was filled with troops, but fortunately the enemy did not do more than throw a few shells into it occasionally, and did not heavily bombard it until the majority of the troops had gone away. Among the features of this life which remain in one's memory are the good baths, mentioned in earlier pages, which we had at the deserted brewery beside the Lys Canal, where the huge vats which formerly had brewed that wholesome beverage, beer, were turned to the base use of washing wild and woolly Australians. Surely it was in this spot that Bairnsfather was seized with the inspiration for his well-known sketch, " If you throw in another sardine, Alf, you'll hear from my solicitor ! "

We did not long remain in idleness, but soon commenced those working-parties to Ploegsteert Wood, which, like " the Brook," went on for ever, day and night.

At this period of the war, the Higher Command disdained surprise, and our preparations daily became more marked, and our batteries more numerous, until it seemed, by sight and sound, that there was no room on the landscape for more.

It seemed hardly possible that Fritz could toss anything over without hitting a dump or some other paraphernalia of the artillery. Consequently these " tea-parties" to the woods, breastworks, or Campack Dump, seldom passed uneventfully. On the outgoing and incoming marches, one passed batteries, always, it seemed, in action, from the squat, toad-like heavy howitzers to the barking 18-pounders, and long-suffering as we thought the enemy was, sooner or later he would retaliate, and, to these working parties, he appeared always to pick out the areas through which they were passing, and a tornado is healthy in comparison to an " area shoot " with " cinq-neufs " amongst dumps of live ammunition.

Our 'planes were also very active, and more than once won our admiration by their fearlessness. The occasion when one of our 'planes gave battle to seven Boche aircraft will be remembered, and we all felt genuine sorrow at the death of the unknown airman, who, in flames, did not miss a moat by more than ten feet when he crashed.

It was on the night of 1st-2nd June, that we left Pont de Nieppe behind us, and established ourselves in the subsidiary line at " Maison 1875 " just south of Ploegsteert Wood. The next night the St. Ives sector was taken over, and names such as " Westminster Avenue," " Ash Lane," " St. Andrew's Drive," and " Advanced Estaminet," where Battalion Headquarters was, will bring back varied memories to many. On 3rd June the artillery began preliminary bombardment for the Battle of Messines, and drew heavy retaliation on us, which played havoc with our trenches and C.T.'s, and cost us more than twenty casualties a day. This period before the battle is remarkable for the intense artillery barrages we had continuously to endure, which kept us, when we were not crouching behind our parapets, repairing the damage done to our defences. Much could be said of the spirit of the officers and men that stood this strain. There were also the daylight raids, carried out by units in the division, which were a complete surprise to the enemy, and highly successful.

At 2 a.m. on the 7th June, the battalion was relieved by the assaulting battalions of the 9th and 10th Brigades, who filed into the assembly trenches of this sector for the attack on Messines Ridge. This relief remains an indelible picture in the minds of all who participated, as it was carried out under extremely dramatic conditions, a heavy artillery bombardment, consisting mostly of gas, raging at the time. Without intermission, with that whistling sound peculiar to gas, the shells rained in along the front, and Ploegsteert Wood was white with chlorine and H.E. The Wood itself in this storm was a scene of wild confusion, where masked ingoing and outgoing troops, carrying-parties, wounded, staff, and working-parties jostled each other in their semi-blindness. In spite of what has been said against the discipline of the Australians, which allegations, by the way, are hardly compatible with the truth, it was the discipline and training, and the keenness of all ranks not to "let a cobber down" that enabled this tangled skein to straighten itself out, and the troops to carry out their allotted tasks to time. No sooner was the relief completed and the battalion settled in the subsidiary line at Maison 1875, than we were reorganised into carrying-parties to take up ammunition, food, water, and engineering material to the captured line. At zero hour, 3.10 a.m., our artillery put down a perfect barrage, after firing four large mines on the Divisional front, the explosion of which was heard for miles. History gives full particulars of this great tactical success. As soon as word was received that the "black" line had been captured, our carrying-parties set out, and it can be said, to the credit of those engaged in this dangerous work, that in spite of heavy artillery shelling, these parties ran the gauntlet continuously and despite heavy casualties never failed to deliver the material entrusted to them at its rightful destination. Under these unhealthy conditions, we also put down a buried cable, which nobody was sorry to see completed. The following officers distinguished themselves during this period, and were afterwards thanked by the Corps Commander :— Lieutenants G. S. Taylor, G. C. C. Wilson, K. A. Murdoch, and T. Wright. On the 9th we changed our quarters to the catacombs, where we carried out our duties until four days later, when we were relieved and moved back to bivouacs at Hillside Camp near Neuve Eglise. Amid the grimness of war, little incidents of humour continually crop up, some of which are worth repeating. One may call to mind the Duffey incident. No. 2062 Private E. C. Duffey, afterwards killed (26th June), came across a captured whizz bang gun, when leading a party somewhere in that shell-torn waste east of Messines. He was immediately seized with the idea of assisting in the barrage work, without going through the formalities required by the C.R.A. Bringing the gun to bear on that tempting target Warneton, the weapon was loaded, and five promptly sat on the trail to steady her. Fortunately for the five on the trail, before "bombardier" Duffey could find the firing lever an officer appeared on the scene and enquired what they were doing? "Strafing Fritz," said Duffey. "What is your name?" was the next question. "Oh, I don't want any decoration for this," answered our friend, who scented trouble, and he and his aspirant gunners promptly decamped. Another tale told of this period is about a certain gentleman in "D" Company, who gets "mentioned" in later pages. Being in the unfortunate position of having taken a prisoner without rifle and bayonet, he did the only reasonable thing to a right-thinking man in asking his mates for a loan of their instruments of aggression to despatch the intruder. On his request being refused by his mates, who could not see eye to eye with him in the matter, Rogers—it will out—made such statements regarding them and those that preceded them, as would have made the sergeant-major blush. Finding that this frenzied eloquence was wasted on his mates, the disgusted Rogers, with the Boche at heel like a retriever, souvenired pill-boxes in the vicinity, and insisted on his "find" tasting sundry liquors and edibles, to see that they had no ill effects, before they themselves partook thereof. This very "fed-up" Hun was at length rescued by an officer and sent back to the prisoners' cage.

We rested and reorganised at Neuve Eglise for a few days, and then moved back to Blanche Maison, a stone's throw from Steenwerck, where the battalion was billeted in the surrounding farm-houses. During the week we stayed here, great attention was given to specialist training, Lewis gun, signalling, bombing and scouting. Also, on the ground opposite Battalion Headquarters, we held a sports meeting, which was one of the most enjoyable gatherings the battalion has ever known. At this time the cherry trees were laden with their red luscious fruit, and many, to improve their scouting, no doubt, carried out "silent raids"—usually with fruitful results. On the 21st June our spell came to an end, and at 4 a.m. we moved past Steenwerck Station, with its huge dump of engineering material, to Hillside Camp.

An incident at Messines — June 1917

CHAPTER 2

Holding the Line on Messines Ridge.—Mud and Shell Holes.—Nature of Sector.—Outpost Fighting and Heavy Shelling.—A Typical Working-party.—Major A. R. Heron, D.S.O., assumes Command of the Battalion.—Camp in La Douve Valley.

At sundown we moved out of Hillside Camp and wended our way through the vehicle-crowded streets of Neuve Eglise—the backwash of the big offensive—to the historic Messines Ridge. Before Messines was reached, guides from the battalion that we were relieving (the Cheshires) met us, and in the fading light took us over the hill. During the approach march, the enemy, as usual, searched the roads with 5.9's, which kept one alert, especially when halting at the ten minutes to the hour. On the ridge itself we found things not exactly homelike, the enemy having taken a special dislike to the place since he lost it, and never ceasing to dispense his favours with a liberal hand. In the darkness one went blindly forward, wandering round gaping shell-holes, where a glimpse of water could be caught in the sheen of Verey Lights, lost to surroundings, and wondering dimly how much further off the destination was. At last, disdaining communication trenches, waist deep in mud and water, the front line was reached, and having completed the relief, the garrisons selected the driest spots to accommodate themselves.

The first night in a new sector is never an inspiring experience, as the familiarity with places which one soon acquires is lacking, and strange to say, even if one's sector is frequently the object of artillery strafes, a thorough knowledge of the locality seems to imbue one with a sense of security. Just a few words about this sector, which may help to bring to the reader's mind the times he spent there, with its many discomforts and dangers. On the right (where at time of writing) "C" company abode, the La Douve River, which in Australia we would never be guilty of calling anything but a creek, flowed to its junction with the Lys at Warneton.

Warneton—now held strongly by the enemy—already showed signs of war-weariness, only equalled by Messines, which rose gaunt in the skyline in our rear, a silent city of shell-torn buildings. Our line, which was practically at the foot of the gentle slopes of Messines, ran past the level farm De la Croix with its garden hedge and row of trees still intact, though perhaps slightly bent, and on towards Hun Walk, where we joined the 42nd Battalion. Incidentally the members of "D" Company will remember vividly Farm de la Croix, with a silent Hun, helmeted complete, sitting with his back against a tree. To all visitors he was pointed out as a good Hun. There was also a certain dump of German gas shells, which peacefully slumbered at the corner of the garden except when a chance shell woke them up and necessitated the adjustment of gas-masks. As Farm de la Croix is remembered by "D" Company, so will the members of "B" have recollections of Horseshoe Lagoon with its broken aeroplane, where they toiled at night, putting down a new line in "No Man's Land," trying in vain to check the inward flow of water. "C" Company also had its familiar spot in the paved road running into the farm, where, from behind our breastworks, a good view of the dug-outs along the La Douve and "No Man's Land"—that vision of tangled wire, shell-holes and broken trenches—could be obtained. Within an hour of our arrival the New Zealanders on our right started the ball rolling, and drew heavy retaliation on our line, especially in the vicinity of Farm de la Croix. "D" Company suffered particularly heavy casualties, among the killed being Sergeant McCafferty, whilst Major E. J. Christoe and Lieutenant Dimmock were amongst the wounded. The next night the companies in the front line, having first of all thrown out covering parties, advanced into "No Man's Land," and commenced digging a new line, which was completed during the ensuing night. The second night at this work was notable. "B" Company made their appearance over the top before the last rays of light had departed, and the enemy, fearing an attack, put up an S.O.S. which was ably answered by his artillery, and the other companies, who were forced to leave their trenches and take shelter from the bombardment in "No Man's Land," had more excitement than was good for them. This new line was practically a blessing in disguise, as every night the enemy, to keep us out of mischief, would periodically drop a "hate" on to our trenches, which of course were unoccupied. Throughout the eighteen days we were in front of Messines we held the front line alternately with the 43rd Battalion, retiring to trenches when in support in front of Bethlehem Farm and White Spot Cottage. When settled near Bethlehem Farm, men of "D" Company will remember the doings of one cook—Rodger. A peculiarity of Rodger was to divide the A.I.F. into two classes, either you were an officer, in which case you were entitled, irrespective of rank, to the prefix Mr., or else you were a "digger." That is by the way. On the same principle on which Mahomet acted in respect to the mountain Rodger souvenired a German boiler, came forward to the vicinity of his company, and took up his quarters among the debris of what had once been a farm-house. Judge of the Hun's displeasure when they saw a column of smoke rising from the ruins that marked Rodger's Cookhouse! Day and night they "hated" that place, but by a miracle did not hit it, and until ordered back by Battalion Headquarters the cook supplied hot steaming tea to cold and weary working-parties after their toil was done. Whether in the front line or supports all men except Lewis gunners were on working-parties every night. As soon as darkness fell, and landmarks lost their definite shape and assumed in one's imagination a foelike form, the order would be heard " No. —— Platoon get ready for a working party." Usually one's interest would not go so far as to enquire what form of toil was expected of one that night. Helping each other up, we would scramble in the mud of the parados and stretch ourselves, assuming " the prone," careless of the consequences of mud, or an empty bully-beef tin scratching one's countenance, when the rat-a-tat-tat of a Boche machine gun traversing the line would strike a new note in the never-silent air. One soon learnt to know by the zip-zip of the bullets when he had passed on, but alas! a sudden switch back on his tracks had often left gaps in the ranks of working parties. The party is ready to move, the last man is helped up by an irate N.C.O., who breathes reflections on the offender's ancestors. It is strange how one man in a platoon will be invariably late, at the last moment he cannot find his pick, or shovel, or rifle. The fates seem to be always against him, poor chap, and incidentally the platoon always has to wait for him. At last our late friend is ready, and muttering something about having left his pipe in the fire-bay, he takes his place in the procession. There moves off in single file a party laden down like unto pack mules, carrying in addition to all arms and equipment a pick or shovel and duckboard, or " A " Frame. It is not very difficult to keep one's direction towards the front line, as " No Man's Land," thanks to the enemy, is brightly illuminated.

In Flanders during 1917, all along the front, one could see any night without, however, fully appreciating the sight, finer pyrotechnical displays than ever celebrated the birthday of monarchs, or the dawn of Peace. Verey Lights of all colours and descriptions would be seen in the air at the same time, now soaring skywards to burst a second later into Pleiades-like clusters, now again remaining gracefully poised like arclights, to grow gradually dimmer, but before expiration to be replaced by many others of equal brightness. Towards this apparent Fairyland, the platoon, skirting the edge of yawning shell-holes, and stumbling through broken trenches and barbed wire, with muttered curses would make its way. Often the enemy would commence to strafe the area immediately in front, and the platoon, without any word of command, would melt away into shell-holes, and philosophically lighting a " fag," wait until the Hun transferred his activities elsewhere. Sometimes the platoon was unfortunate, and the stretcher-bearers were to the fore, and the party filling sandbags or digging trenches was more silent than was their wont. Half an hour before daybreak, with more animattion than hitherto shown, the party would turn their steps homewards, and, if fortunate, would secure a cup of hot tea before turning-in to sleep with the dawning light.

Now that our troubles are over, and we live in comfort, not many thoughts are wasted on the privations we endured at this period. Seldom a day or night passed that did not bring rain, and rain in trenches, especially unrevetted ones, is, to say the least, a misery. Many readers will have painful recollections of trying to steal a few hours' sleep, sitting on a bayonet stuck into the slimy side of the trench, with groundsheet wound round the steel helmet and laced up the front, while one's feet, long since numb with cold, sank deeper in the mud and water. It would be doing them an injustice if the Pioneers were not mentioned. Although chiefly renowned for the comfort they can gather round in their billets a little tale is related of them during this period. After one of our patrols had killed a Boche the pioneers were detailed to bury the body, as the "pard" was otherwise engaged. Selecting a large shell-hole, the pioneer corporal said, "We'll give him a bit of a burial service." The others, taking him at his word, "dipped their lids." The corporal, picking up some earth, repeated the following: "Earth to earth, ashes to ashes—I wish there were a thousand instead of one of you blighters—Push him in, Jim."

This tour of the line, saw a complete change in the Battalion Headquarters. On the morning of the 7th July, while the officers were gathered around the festive board, a 105 m.m. shell came into the dug-out, and killed Lieutenant Fern, the artillery liaison officer, and wounded Lieutenant-Colonel F. J. Board, Major Kinnish, Captain Chumleigh, and Lieutenants MacGibbon and Dodds, besides wounding some signallers. We were all genuinely sorry to lose our C.O., who returned to Australia without seeing the battalion again. As the Second in Command, Major T. A. Ferguson, was attending a senior officers' course in England, Major A. R. Heron, D.S.O. (42nd Battalion) was sent over to take command, and the battalion can congratulate itself on its good fortune in this respect, as the efficiency of the 41st, as a fighting unit and the happy relationship existing between the officers and men all bear witness to his tireless efforts and excellent example.

Before ending this phase, one must mention the pleasure all ranks felt when our padre, Captain-Chaplain Mills, received the coveted "Military Cross," the first chaplain in the Division to receive this decoration. Day and night, notwithstanding what the Boche was throwing over, the padre ran his "cocoa joint," and administered hot drinks to wounded and weary men, and any who have seen him burying the dead, will always remember the magnificent serenity which never allowed even close-bursting shells to interrupt his devotions over the fallen. Amongst our glorious dead, who lie on the slopes of Messines, are Lieutenants A. Dickie, T. G. Taylor, G. C. C. Wilson, and L. Wellings.

On being relieved by our 9th Brigade, we moved back to a camp in the La Douve Valley, where the customary overhauling and re-equipping took place. It is worthy of mention that at a Brigade Sports held at this time, the battalion won the Brigade Cup, securing more points in the aggregate than the other three battalions put together. This was largely brought about by the fine performance put up by No. 2770 L.-Corporal C. E. White.

CHAPTER 3.

Plans for New Offensive.—Return to Messines Sector.—Attack of the 31st of July, 1917.—More Mud.—The Great Machine Gun Barrages in Front of Warneton.—Out to De Seule Camp.

We had not long been out on this rest before the signs portended that at an early date we should see the line again.

We will endeavour to describe briefly the share we were asked to take in the big attack which was to be made from the Lys northward to the sea, which, by the way, did not turn out a success, although we and the troops on our immediate flanks did all that was desired of them.

The scheme was as follows:—On the 31st of July the brigade was to capture German posts in "No Man's Land" west of Warneton, establish posts ourselves on our sector of operations, and go far enough forward to give the enemy the impression that Warneton was our objective. At the same time this forward party would act as a protection to the digging of these posts. On the posts being captured, consolidated, and connected laterally and to the rear by the 42nd and 43rd Battalions, the 44th and 41st Battalions were to man and hold them. We practised hard, and all ranks were made conversant with the whole scheme, so that intelligent assistance could be given, and on the night 29th-30th of July we retraced our steps to the sector we had last vacated.

During the following day the battalion was subjected to very heavy shelling. That night the 43rd Battalion came in and relieved us, and we moved back to trenches, slightly in rear, where we remained throughout the next day. At 3.50 a.m. July 31st the attack broke out along the whole front, and in the inferno attendant thereon the 43rd with the 42nd on the left went forward. On the right, the New Zealand Brigade captured La Basseville, which they held in spite of herculean efforts by the Boche to wrest it from them. It was nearly two hours before we received any information, and then came a spectacle which later on was to become so familiar—strings of muddy, bloodstained prisoners, of perhaps five to twenty each, with a slightly wounded " Digger " as escort, smoking the inevitable " fag "—testifying to the fact that the attack was progressing favourably. One Boche wounded, ticketed for hospital by his Medical Service, chose ours instead, and, dodging our snipers, surrendered to us with the greatest outward satisfaction. Later on, we heard definitely that the attack had succeeded, and three posts—vii., viii., and ix.—been established. Owing to the heavy casualties sustained, the task of connecting up the posts and digging communication trenches was not carried out. In almost total darkness we relieved the 43rd. While the relief was still in progress word came through that the redoubtable " Windmill," Post viii., had been recaptured. An immediate counter-attack was organized, in which a platoon of the 41st participated, and the post was reoccupied. The officers in charge of the posts were: Lieutenant W. M. McLean, who received the Military Cross for his valuable and gallant work, vii.; Lieutenant P. H. Harrison, viii.; and Lieutenant E. D. Price, ix.

The period which followed was the most trying that the battalion had yet had to face, and was also perhaps one of the worst it ever experienced in France. On that night it began to rain heavily, and kept on almost continuously during our occupancy of the line. The condition of the ground was truly awful. The trenches were waist-high in water, in which the few gum-boots we possessed were valueless. The garrisons of the posts had a particularly trying time. It was impossible to improve their positions, as the ground fell in as fast as it was dug, and as no communication trenches could be made for the same reason, the posts were isolated during the hours of daylight. A finer example of dogged tenacity could not be found than in those heroes' display. For six days, wet through to the skin, with hardly any hot food or sleep, and with rifles and Lewis guns in many cases clogged with mud, they beat off repeated determined enemy counter-attacks. Many men during the day fell asleep standing up, and it is not to be wondered at that the sick rate went up, and that platoons, thirty-five strong originally, came out in many cases with only five men. The enemy shelling was very severe, and on the 3rd of August Lieutenant E. D. Price was shell-shocked, and evacuated. His post was taken over by Sergeant R. Goodwin, who in later battles was to win the " M. M." and bar. It was originally understood that we were to be relieved on the night of 2nd-3rd of August, but this did not eventuate till two nights later. On the night 2nd-3rd August two companies of the 39th Battalion were sent up to try to connect up the posts, as we were too weak to attempt it ourselves. They were unsuccessful; they might just as well have tried to work in quicksand. The next night these two companies were definitely handed over to us to strengthen the garrisons, and we withdrew our personnel, which was exhausted. The covering barrages dropped by the artillery and machine guns will never be forgotten, especially that by the latter. Situated in ideal positions for most effective employment, these weapons, some sixty-eight to a frontage of 1,000 yards, before the " golden rain " S.O.S. had time to burst, put down a fence of lead which few of the enemy penetrated alive. All will remember the morning we allowed the enemy to come in to " No Man's Land " to collect his dead and wounded. This, to the uninitiated, seems the only humane thing to do, but when one is dealing with an enemy who seldom respects the Red Cross flag, and who in fact looks on a stretcher party as a splendid target, one's sense of humanity becomes strangely distorted. At last we were relieved by a battalion of New Zealanders, and behind Messines we embussed in motor-lorries, which took us to De Seule Camp, which was situated between Neuve Eglise and Steenwerck. The men were so exhausted that they had to be assisted out of the lorries, but after a few days' rest they had practically recovered their former vivacity.

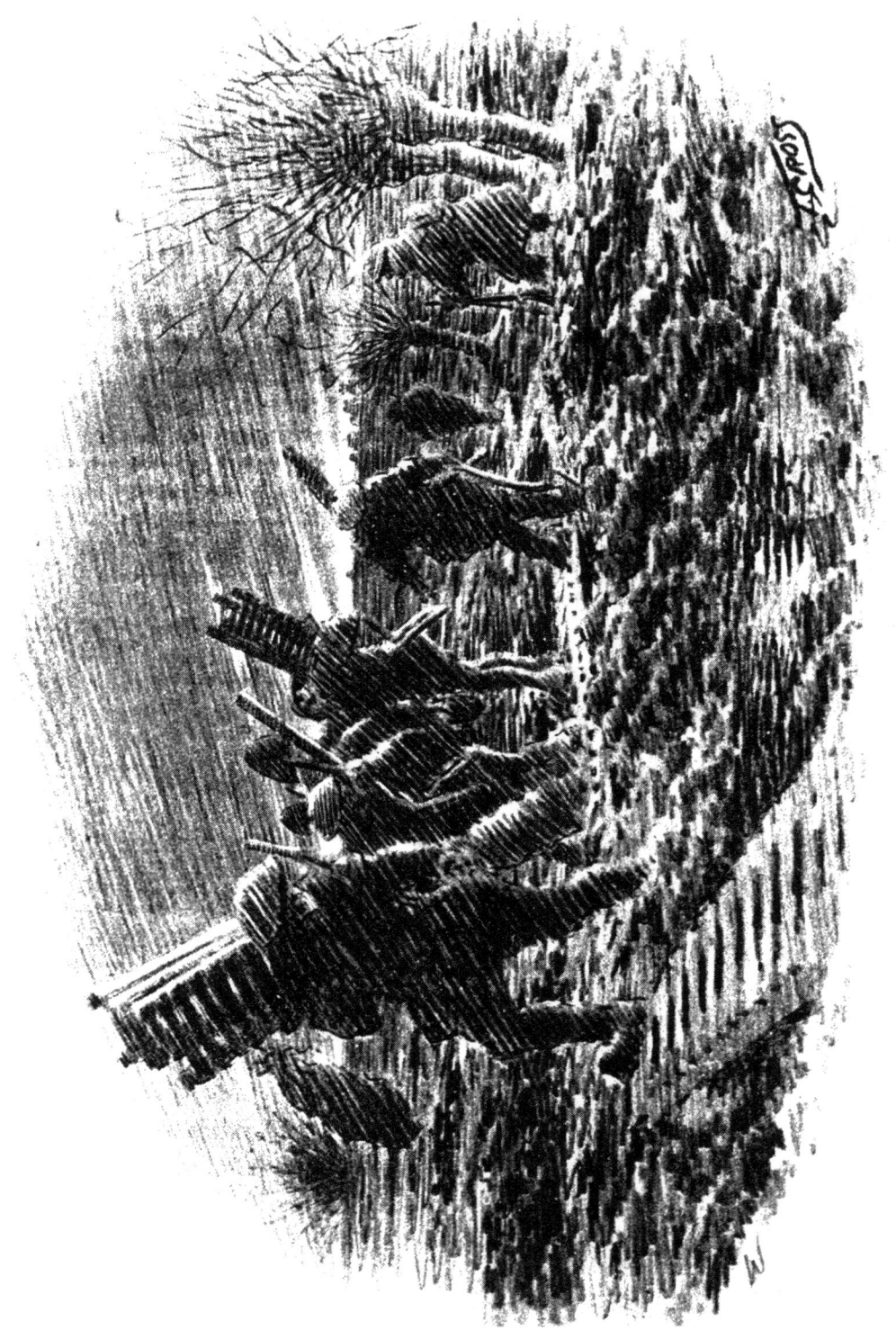

Working Party – Messines 1917.

PHASE IV.

CHAPTER I.

Going Back for a Spell.—Ste. Marie Capelle.—Assinghem : The Paper Mill.—A Practice Stunt.—Third Division Reviewed by Sir Douglas Haig.—Three Days' March to Poperinghe.—Gothas, Bombs, and Chows.

On the 15th August we moved out from De Seule Camp, and reached Steenwerck, where we entrained for Hazebrouck. From Hazebrouck we marched to Ste. Marie Capelle, that picturesque little village nestling below Cassel. All will have pleasant recollections of this place, with its cleanly billets, and the kindly, hospitable inhabitants, who treated us so well. During this month Lieutenant R. F. Pickering came over from the 42nd, to be our energetic Adjutant.

For a week we stayed here. Meanwhile we continued our training, and on one day held a sports meeting. It was with genuine regret that we left this spot, never to return, and marched to Hazebrouck.

On detraining at Wizernes, we resumed our march, and reached our billeting-places—Plouy, Campagnette, and Fordebecque—late in the afternoon. Nobody enjoyed the latter part of the march with full packs and blankets. The first big hill stretching up from Wizernes, and the heat of the day, took all pleasure away, and our enjoyment was not further increased when, having thrown aside our packs, we entered into possession of our billets.

The contrast to Ste. Marie Capelle was strongly marked. The billets were crowded and dirty. In many cases the pigs and calves were turned out to make room, and the rain, commencing to fall, still further added to our discomfort. "B" Company, who stayed at Plouy, encountered one of those minor tragedies which are sent to try us. Arriving at their billets, tired and thirsty, with empty water-bottles, they clustered round the only well available. The genius on the windlass caught the first bucketful on the side of the well and broke the rope. As the well was deep, and it was a long wait for the water-carts, everybody was so pleased, and the culprit received many benedictions.

It was therefore with the greatest satisfaction that we left these billets to their rightful owners three days later, and marched to Assinghem. Here practically the whole battalion was billeted in an old paper-mill on the banks of the River Aa. The billets were clean, though perhaps rather cold, being of stone, but on straw being supplied the men settled down in fair comfort. During the month spent here, we carried out systematic training for the battle which we knew was in front of us, although when or where this effort was to take place we knew not.

Beside thorough specialist training, we carried out practice-attacks in open and semi-open warfare, finishing, as all will remember, with the customary bayonet charge uphill to the Plouy road.

The nature of these practice-attacks was new to us. Heretofore the tasks laid down were to capture and hold certain enemy trenches. The idea we were now working on was to follow and mop up behind a barrage, and capture the area of ground, irrespective of trenches, up to the covering barrage. One is inclined to think that these practices were not disliked, for all ranks were keen then, and not even the most hardened "turnip-chewer" did much growling. We carried out this work before the Corps, Divisional, and Brigade Commanders, who gave us the benefit of their experience in helpful criticism.

On a certain day in September, 1917, the N.C.O.'s of the battalion, probably by prearranged plan, tramped noisily back and forth among the sleeping troops, who stirred protestingly and uttered many rude remarks. It may have been that these N.C.O.'s had so great a sense of their grave responsibilities that sleep was impossible for them. At any rate, when *reveille* sounded, up and down the rows of sleepers they rushed, yelling the old parrot cries, "Rise and shine; show a leg," and then the conviction came to all that the great stunt, rumours of which had passed round the day before, was really to take place, for never, except on really important occasions, does *reveille* sound at or about midnight. Were they glad, these heroes of Messines? Perhaps. One thing is certain. They were determined to get it over as quickly as possible. At "Cook-house" an eager crowd gathered round the cookers, for one must go into a stunt well fortified. Haversacks were filled with biscuits, cheese, and bully, as an additional precaution. Then came the order, "All right, get out on parade." All got there, after struggling for a while to fix equipment in the latest fashion. It may be mentioned by no means the least serious of the problems confronting the Divisional Staff is that of determining the mode of wearing the web-equipment, and the resultant praises of the various important persons who inspect and review us at irregular intervals is surely sufficient justification for the continuation of such weighty deliberations. Arrived on parade the battalion was closely scrutinized, and every man made ready for the struggle. Each platoon commander passed to his platoon the information that would enable them to carry out successfully their allotted share in the operations. After two hours' standing on parade, the battalion moved off, to the evident satisfaction of the men. For an hour we marched by platoons in columns of fours, two hundred yards between platoons, then two deep, and finally advanced to the scene of the proposed operation in single file. Here it was that the cunning resource of the Intelligence Officer received a severe test, for the route was new to him; but he rose to the occasion, and, by constant reference to his trusty and much-mauled map, succeeded in bringing us to a position known as the "jumping-off line," without our being observed by the enemy. We took up dispositions as ordered and waited for "zero hour," which, contrary to all precedent, was fixed for 10 a.m. We read in books of the attitude of men during the period of waiting. They are pictured as moving restlessly, white-faced, and obviously thoroughly imbued with a sense of the responsibility resting on their coming efforts. Few—a very few—appear calm; others joke to hide the uncontrollable nervousness that at such times comes to all except a very few. No man who was there for that stunt would see those things in our faces. We talked frivolously of trivial things, and those not talking were listening. Such weighty matters as these they talked of :—Which "boozer" kept the best rum, beer, vin blanc, or Malaga; discipline, ability of cooks and quality of "tucker"; the duration of the war, M. M.'s and their recipients, the "heads," and deserters. For example— "One day in the training camp the guard bring in a bloke dressed pretty swanky in "civvies" and a "pee wee" hat. He had been handed over to the Colonel, because he answered the description of a Light Horse "bloke" who had been adrift from Egypt for two years. He kept the tale to himself, and the Colonel could not get anything out of him, so he awarded fourteen days C.B., and put him on the strength of one of the companies, till further orders as to his disposal should be received. The bloke had tea with us. He didn't have breakfast." At 9.55 officers became fidgety, and kept eyes on wristlet watches, so that the whole battalion might "hop over" simultaneously. At length the tension was broken by the blasts of one hundred whistles, sounded in a medley of keys. Over we hopped, and walked steadily on, protected by a fine artillery barrage. We had gone, perhaps one hundred yards, when the first casualty occurred; he was shot through an arm and leg, but was cheerful almost to exuberance. "Carry on, boys," he said, "same as if I were there." It is indicative of the fine spirit always exhibited by our wounded, that right through that terrible advance their cheerfulness was most marked, and went a long way towards bucking us up. "After all," we thought, "it can't hurt very much." Each man carried a pick or shovel, and when the objective was reached, and incidentally all enemy resistance overcome, we proceeded to "dig in." We had not dug very deeply, when our Brigadier rode up and gave the word to close. It was high time too. Most of us had left ground-sheets behind in billets, and by that time were thoroughly wet.

We "closed," and marched to the cookers, but none wished to eat until dry, so we were taken "home." In the subsequent discussion in the shelter of the old mill, one person, on being asked his opinion of the "stunt," remarked that he doubted if the knowledge gained by the "heads" in their endeavours to choose the best formations for future attacks in the line was sufficient justification for the crops ruined during the stunt, which of course had to be paid for. On the 22nd September, after brushing up our boots, and the usual "eye wash," we marched to Drionville. The whole 3rd Division was here inspected by the Commander-in-Chief, Sir Douglas Haig. The inspection passed off well, except for the Brigadier's not watching a certain pennant being raised and lowered, but no doubt the subsequent movements of the troops were at least unique. These inspections are auguries of ill omen, as there are usually "hop overs" to follow these "pattings on the back." On the 26th we moved out of Assinghem, leaving it cleaner than it had ever been in the memory of its oldest inhabitants. French villages may have godliness, and of this we have our doubts, but they certainly do not practise the principles of cleanliness. For the next three days we route-marched northwards, billeting the two nights at Blaringhem and Eecke. Speaking of billeting, do you remember your first experiences, when, with very limited French at your disposal, you approached the ample Madame for shelter under her roof? Perhaps you will remember how you waited till the "barrage lifted," and again put in your simple question, until finally the voluble householder, out of breath, signified her willingness to come to terms. But to resume our narrative: these route marches are never experiences to glory in, especially when, as in this case, men have been inoculated the day previous. Marching with all one's belongings on one's back, through mud and mire, or over cobbled roads with their uneven surfaces, is not conducive to pleasure, and reaching in the dark billets, mostly dirty, crowded, and uncomfortable, which are left again at daylight, does not tend to alter one's feelings in this respect. All therefore were pleased, when, after passing along one of the finest roads lined with trees we had yet seen, the lofty spire of Poperinghe rose before us. On arrival at Poperinghe we camped just south of the town in tents, at what was known as "Camp 30." Poperinghe at this time still had a fair number of civilians dwelling there, in spite of occasional shelling, and more than occasional night-bombing. For the ensuing four days officers and N.C.O.'s made reconnaissances of the front astride the Ypres-Zonnebeke Railway as far forward as possible. In open fields also, among the hop poles, the battalion practised attack formations and what we call "hanging to a barrage"; the barrage in these cases represented by flags. On a grassy plot adjacent to the camp a replica to scale of the final objective was made, where common or garden objects, representing known strong points, pill-boxes, &c., gave all a good idea of the country we were to

Caught and held — Ypres — 1917.

operate on. The weather at this period was fine, with bright moonlight nights, which tempted the enemy bombing-'planes to visit us. One might mention that we had no protection against bombs, in the shape of revetting or trenches to take cover in. It was no unusual occurrence to see, until two or three in the morning, small groups outside their tents watching the bursts of "Archies," and streams of "tracers" searching in vain for the intruders. One night a shout of joy went up from the spectators when a shell burst, seemingly, under the tail of a Gotha; but alas! he soared on, and soon the crunch, crunch, crunch, and the red flashed skywards showed that he had dropped his cargo. We were very fortunate. The camp beside us suffered half a hundred casualties in one night. There was that night, never to be forgotten, when a Gotha distributed its favours in the vicinity of the Chinese encampment, a few hundred yards up the road. Not heeding the barbed wire surrounding the camp, its inmates in déshabille burst through like a herd of bullocks, and, with the air resonant with "Wha' for," made for the four winds of heaven. Many sought shelter up trees and in haystacks, and it took distracted gendarmes for miles around all the following day to collect and conduct this branch of humanity back to its dwelling-place.

CHAPTER 2.

Ypres.— 4th October, 1917, Battle of Broodseinde.—The 41st Over the Top.—The Terrific Barrage.—Toronto Camp.—Return to Ypres.—In Front of Paschendaele.—The Sea of Mud.—Scenes of Death and Desolation.—Back to Assinghem.

It was early in the morning of the 3rd October that we left camp to entrain at Brandhoek Siding. As a Unit we entered Ypres for the first time, and detrained at the Asylum—perhaps an appropriate place—and bivouacked on the ground beside the cemetery on the Menin road. One will never forget one's first impression of the most historical city of the war—Ypres. This was the first large town we had seen the victim of "Kultur," and even the first dreams we had of this place, when we heard it was to be our fighting sector, did not come up to reality. Ypres, with its silent streets and stricken houses, which once throbbed with the life of a laughter-loving people, will for ever remain in our memories. It stands a monument for all time to the thousands who lie round it beneath little white crosses; they who, by their noble self-sacrifice, prevented the enemy from ever treading its streets. Here, as at Messines, was the bustle of all arms co-operating for the success of what was officially known as the third phase of the third battle of Ypres, or the battle of Broodseinde. This battle was fought on a frontage of 10 miles, and the Australians were given the place of honour in the centre. The 3rd Division attacked along the Ypres-Zonnebeke Railway, with the 2nd Division on the south and the New Zealand Division on the north. The battle was a tactical one, with limited objectives along the Broodseinde Ridge. It was intended from here to capture the Paschendaele Ridge, but the severity of the weather made it impossible for the troops who participated in the third phase to carry out this task. At 11 p.m., after a hot meal, the advance march began. Picking our way amongst the débris and shell-holes along the railway embankment, under desultory shelling, we reached the viaduct. Here we had to lie up for an hour while assembly-tapes were put out. The front was by no means quiet, and this hour, spent under continuous shelling, is numbered amonst the longest ever passed by many. At length a further move forward to Bremen Redoubt was made, and although the assembly-place was here, it was thought inadvisable to stay, so we moved across the Zonnebeke River. In crossing we had at least thirty casualties. We had to run the gauntlet of a heavy area shoot on the three duckboard bridges which spanned this waste of mud and water, and two out of three were destroyed under our feet. Shelter was taken in shell-holes in rear of the three battalions who were to take the first three objectives. Our role was the taking of the fourth and final one. On our left assembled the 10th and on our right the 7th Brigade. A battalion from the same State, " Sunny Queensland," the 26th, was accompanying us on our right to the final objective. In this goodly company we, not forgetting four luckless mules with water, awaited Zero Hour. Half an hour after we arrived (5.30 a.m.) the Germans put down an intense barrage, which fortunately fell mostly on the Zonnebeke and Bremen Redoubts in rear of us. Rain commenced to fall steadily. In waterlogged shell-holes, all longed for the hour of action to arrive. Prompt to the second, at 6 a.m. the British barrage dropped with the sound of thunder. Perhaps never in the history of this war was there such a concentration of artillery in one place as in the Ypres salient at this period. It was impossible to pick out the sound of any one gun ; the air was filled with a dull roar, and a scene such as Dante in his " Inferno " could not have imagined was unfolded. Stretching away on both flanks, further than the eye could see, was nothing but pulsating waves of red and white and purple, belching forth a whirlwind of death in front of our advancing infantry. After three minutes of this—Furies let loose—the gathering of troops along the front moved forward, and we with them. The attack commenced in darkness. In the Hades, all recognised formations went by the board, and " columns of lumps " picked their way forward, recking nought of casualties caused by the enemy barrage. Although actually our share in the fighting was not to commence until the other three battalions had captured their objectives, our more adventurous spirits pushed forward with the leading waves, and participated in all the fighting that came their way. All opposition was completely overcome. By the time the memorable Hill 40 was left behind, the majority of the men going forward were smoking German cigars, taken from " pill-boxes." The casual character of the Australian was borne out by many an incident that occurred, such as the following :—At the second halt of the barrage, to enable the 42nd Battalion to consolidate, four of our men, unmindful of the drama being enacted before their eyes, were seen sitting in a shell-hole playing " show-poker " for souvenired coins. The first two objectives were taken by the 43rd and 42nd Battalions. After the second objective was passed the " going " was very bad, especially north of the railway line. In a quagmire of mud knee-deep and tangled barbed wire, we lost the barrage, and after very heavy losses carried the objective at the point of the bayonet. It was at this period that 2nd Lieutenant W. A. Fraser, who had already performed many acts of gallantry, attacked a pill-box which was holding up his platoon, and single-handed either killed or took prisoner the occupants numbering at least thirty. For this he received the " D.S.O." An interesting study in an offensive is the tide coming back. No sooner, it seems, are our infantry in the enemy trenches, than the tangible result is seen in the hordes of prisoners which emerge therefrom. These groups, like frightened sheep, make their way back with wounded in their midst, and their escort, usually a wounded man, being helped back by a Boche. One seldom saw a prisoner not carrying something, either a spare pair of boots, a dixie, or " hunk " of unappetising bread, evidently the first things he could lay his hands on. These men, all along the route, would be pressed into service for conveying wounded by our harassed stretcher-bearers. Along this trail would also travel our slightly wounded, in apparent brotherhood with stray prisoners, and all invariably smoking, either from habit, or on account of the multitudinous unburied dead. Amongst this melee moved alert runners, carrying back news of the attack, and easily distinguishable by the red bands on their arms.

One will remember vividly our line above Dash Crossing, where lies that gallant and ever-cheerful soldier, Captain J. Redmond, who was killed by a shell after consolidation was completed. Astride the railway on the left with the Lewis gun post in the cutting, " D " Company had their position. Along the ridge, amid old Boche trenches, ran " C " Company's line, with " A " Company on its right. " A " Company's sector included a road junction, with signboards still intact, and they also had a platoon from the 26th Battalion in their midst. Soon after this line was taken the Germans massed for a counter attack, but before it could be launched a party consisting of men of "B" and "C" Companies, under Lieutenant Skewes, by a brilliant bayonet charge, routed them. Unfortunately that brave officer was killed, and Lieutenant C. H. Butler. who went forward to recover the body, wounded.

Throughout the day, repeated counter attacks were made, the cemetery on the left flank being the favourite, and one might say the appropriate, spot to assemble in. All efforts were frustrated by Lewis gun, rifle, and trench-mortar fire, and for the attack, which assumed larger proportions, we called in the aid of the artillery with the S.O.S. rocket—red over green over yellow. A tale is told about 2218, Private H. Peacock. This energetic young man found himself in advance of our barrage, and took shelter in a pill-box, where he came upon a party of five Huns. Not in the least abashed, he profitably filled in his time, until his mates caught up to him, by souveniring these flowers of the German army. On reaching our line of consolidation, his mate, J. Watters, was killed by a Boche sniper, and Peacock swore revenge. Calling into play all the bush-craft learnt in far-off Wandiligong, Peacock stalked this wily Hun in "No Man's Land," who fired on him without success. When within "assault distance" our friend charged the sniper, who, seeing the game was up, came forward surrendering. Unfortunately for him his overtures for peace were not accepted. The victor returned and buried his pal with his own hands, giving his effects to his platoon officer, Lieutenant M. C. Wood. Six days later this brave man made the supreme sacrifice. Amongst the fallen, the battalion lost Lieutenant John Larkin and the R.M.O., Captain Eric Kerr, both of whom were brave and courteous officers.

We held the line under the usual artillery fire, for which Ypres was noted, until the early morning of the 6th, when we were relieved by the 66th British Division. The Battalion Headquarters for this fight were first at Potsdam, and then in that death-trap of a railway cutting, Alma. The cookers were brought up to the ground adjoining the Asylum, and the hot food put new life into the weary, mudstained men who limped in in groups. After their breakfast many fell asleep from sheer exhaustion. During the day a move back to Toronto Camp was made. By utilising empty motor-lorries returning to Poperinghe it was not necessary to march, and having drawn their blankets the men made themselves comfortable in the Nissen huts, and, with the rain falling outside with dull monotony, were soon lulled to slumber.

Outside the P.O.W. cage at Ypres was gathered a galaxy of "staff," ablaze with red, like any "flame tree." Amongst them was the diggers' bosom pal, the A.P.M. Approaching this august assembly came a miserable undersized specimen of Teutonic origin, covered with mud, and wearing a skullcap with red band, the badge of German infantry, over a countenance of fixed inanity. The cheerful voice of a digger hailed him with : " Are you on the staff, too, Fritz ? "

On the 9th, things not having gone well with the 66th Division, we again marched to Ypres, and bivouacked among the rats and conglomeration of "hows," engineers, and other odds and ends in tumble-down breastworks on the Friezenberg Ridge, which was reached about three in the afternoon. Here, with scanty coverings we carried, we passed the night, and found the ridge true to name. The next morning "we lay doggo," so as not to draw the enemy's attention to our presence. In the afternoon we moved forward in single file along the main Zonnebeke-Ypres road. This road was a congestion of guns, lorries, limbers, pack-mules, horsemen, and parties of all descriptions, and it was truly a miracle that it was left practically unshelled for so long. Once Fritz did start work, of course the traffic thinned down to the minimum, and the crowding ceased. On this occasion we threaded our way through the maze of traffic until Bremen House, a huge pill-box on the right of the road, was reached. Here we branched to the left, and followed the duckboarded "K" track, over Bremen Redoubt, the Zonnebeke, and Hill 40, with its well-known Levi Cottage, Jacob's House, and Van Isaacere Farm, to the marshy river Hanebeek, where, squat in the watery mud of the further bank, nestled Boethoek, where the Battalion Headquarters of the 41st and 42nd were. On over Abraham Heights we went, to the line we were to occupy. All along the route men of the battalion we were relieving were met coming out, so we had no difficulty in finding our destination. In this support position "C" Company took up a line in front of the Grafenstafel switch, where they dug in. "D" Company was associated with the pill-boxes known as "Beecham." "B" Company must have recollections of the swamps at Berlin Wood, where half the company got bogged, and "A" Company's memories will be of Hamburg and Augusta's Wood. The approach was not completed without casualties, and throughout our stay east of Ypres, a matter of thirteen days, we had to pass through heavy artillery-shoots every time we moved. No movement could take place during darkness on account of the heavy state of the ground, which was not only scarred and pitted for miles by countless shells, but was one enormous quagmire, soggy, and waterlogged to such a degree, that to call it a sea of mud would be using the very mildest expression. The landscape was one of desolation—a waste strewn as far as the eye could see with dead, and a confusion of impedimenta of war. All the companies except "C" on Abraham Heights—a place memorable on account of the gassing of the unprotected Canadians in 1915—were unable to dig trenches, and lived in shell-holes, more or less filled with water, which they converted into positions of defence. On the morning of the 13th October, the 9th and 10th Brigades attacked with the New Zealanders on the left, and "A" and "B" Companies came back behind "C" and "D" Companies.

Owing to the New Zealanders being held up by the wire of the Paschendaele-Terhand switch, which included those formidable obstacles, Belle Vue and Crest Farms, the attackers made but little progress, and lost so heavily, that we were ordered, with the 44th on our right, to take over the front line from the 10th Brigade.

In spite of very heavy shelling, the relief was completed by dusk. Before leaving this entry into the line, it is necessary to mention the hard work we had to evacuate the wounded of the 66th Division, whom we found lying in shell-holes and filling all the pill-boxes east of the Hanebeek. Some of the wounded had been lying there from three to four days, and their silence over their sufferings and the thankfulness for the help given to them will long be remembered. This work of humanity under the vile conditions that prevailed told on the men. The front was a strange one to us. On the left, in the hollow, was the Ravebeek, with its marshy banks so distorted by shell-fire that the course of the stream could not be defined.

It being impossible to occupy this country, and it being impassable to the enemy, "C" Company only held the pill-boxes, which stood like white smudges amid the muddy waste of uprooted and mangled trees. The ground from there rose up towards Kerselaar Hoek, and the remaining companies dug trenches in front of that formidable fortification, Dab Trench—that trench of concreted bays and traverses and massive barbed wire entanglements. Behind Dab Trench ran a "pave" road, which the Boche loved to shell, and going along its cobbled way, one felt like a rat in a trap. That little strip of road which ran past Hamburg will never be forgotten by ration-carriers, who involuntarily quickened their pace when on its "holy" surface, and breathed a sigh of relief when it was left behind. Away on the left Crest Farm frowned down upon us, and sniping and machine gunning were frequent from that quarter. For three days we stayed here in the rain and mud, and it was only the innate grit of the men that prevented them from going "sick." Many in their muddy trenches kept their feet in sandbags (as their feet were too swollen with the wet to permit of their wearing their boots) and stuck to their posts through all these privations, which only a soldier ever endures. On coming out we were put in reserves on Hill 40, near Van Isaacere's Farm, with the B.H.Q. in a pill-box on the banks of the Zonnebeke, near where we made our crossing on the 4th October. The position we occupied on Hill 40 was the driest we had so far struck, being on the top of a ridge. The men lost no time in getting below ground, and with their ground-sheets as roofs were fairly comfortable. The first night this position was subjected to a very heavy area-shoot, which lasted for five hours.

The next morning showed the whole area churned up, and although many had their happy homes brought down about their ears, causing no little discomfort and shock to the nerves, our actual casualties were light. Our conditions here were slightly better, except for incessant shelling, and the weather also improved. We filled in our time salvaging military gear that lay around us in profusion.

There is a story worth relating about a burial party.

The Padre, accompanied by some members of Headquarters, was making his usual excursion over captured territory, looking for dead and wounded. Happening to wander over ground taken by New Zealanders the party came upon one severely wounded. The Padre, hoping to save his life, procured a stretcher, and carried him towards the collecting station. After a few yards had been covered, however, the man was dead. Having made certain of this, the Padre announced his intention of seizing the opportunity of burying him. This was done, but under vigorous protests from one of the party, who was firmly convinced that a man was not dead unless cold and stiff. Next day the Padre asked the party to erect a small cross over the grave. When they arrived at the spot, in place of the grave they found a tremendous shell-hole. The superstitious digger remarked, in solemn indignation: "There you are! I knew it; the poor ————'s dug his way out during the night, and crawled away looking for help. Now, perhaps, you'll believe a man." On the evening of the 21st the 50th Canadian Battalion relieved us, and our last impressions of Ypres were shells from the Hun's "rubber gun" bursting amid the ruins of that once fair city as we passed through.

While the relief was in progress, and our tired and laden men filed past Mill Cot, a voice from the darkness asked, "Be ye the West Ridings?" "No," said a fed-up voice, "we're the ———— Anzacs walking." At 10 a.m. next morning we embussed, and, with minds at rest, enjoyed the serenity of a day bright with sunshine. With troops singing from sheer lightheartedness, we passed through Krustraat, Vlamertinghe, Poperinghe, Abeele, Steenvoorde, up the glorious slopes of Cassel, through Arques and Wizernes, till we reached Clety, where we debussed and again occupied our old billets at Assinghem.

The inhabitants were glad to see us, and welcomed us heartily. One can safely say that round estaminet fires, especially the one Gabrielle and Marguerite presided over, feats of valour performed at Ypres lost nothing in the telling, when related in broken French to these ministering angels. The time spent east of Ypres was perhaps one of the most nerve-racking experiences many have undergone. One often hears of the war-look in a man's eyes, but seldom actually sees it. After the days spent in the loathsome mud, with the unburied dead for company, and the never-ceasing bursting shells, the strain gradually produced that haunted war-weary expression on many faces. Even when the hardships of the campaign are forgotten, the mention of the names, such as Abraham's Heights, Boethoek, Berlin Wood, and Hamburg, will never fail to bring back vividly to the memory those scenes of fearful havoc and bleak desolation.

Back from Ypres — October 1917.

PHASE V.

CHAPTER I.

Training at Assinghem.—Long March to Kortepyp.—Voting-day and Bombs.—Kemmel Shelters.—Waterlands Camp near Nieppe.—Christmas, 1917.—Erquinghem and the Working-parties.—Fire Alarms.—Patrolling.—More Working-parties near "Plugstreet."—Holding the Line at Le Bizet.—To Le Romarin and by Train to Quesques.

Assinghem will always bring back many pleasant memories. As far as billets go, the "Old Mill" stands on its own. It served as a barracks for the battalion, and everything was extraordinarily convenient, including a pure and inexhaustible water supply in the River Aa.

The strength of the battalion at this time was under six hundred, but it would have been nothing like this figure after the casualties in October, had not reinforcements come along in fair numbers. Training was fairly ordinary; only the route-marches stand out vividly in the memory. After a fortnight's training, we were again on the march, leaving Assinghem at 8 a.m. on 12th November, and travelling *via* Rebecq, Glomanghem, Rincq, Aire, and Boeseghem to Les Ciseaux, where the battalion billeted for the night. Fortunately the weather was cool, as eighteen miles a day with "house up" will try the best. Resuming the march at 8 a.m. the following morning, most of us feeling somewhat stiff about the shoulders, we passed through Thiennes, Tannay, Croix-Marraiss, Merville, Neuf Berquin, Doulieu, to Noote Boom, a distance of twenty-one miles. In spite of the distance there were no stragglers—surely a marvellous testimony to the spirit of the men, considering what they had lately undergone. The band materially assisted, playing almost continuously toward the close of the march, keeping the minds of all off their weariness. We rested here that night, and also the next day and night. Feeling quite revived after our spell, we were on the road again by 10 a.m. the following morning, passing by way of Labecque and Steenwerck to our destination at Kortepyp. There were huts here—those malthoid affairs; and a very comfortable camp it turned out to be.

The weather had now turned out wintry, fine but cold; really splendid weather for the football matches, which were a great feature of our afternoons here. Besides inter-company matches, the battalion team played matches with the 25th and 26th Battalions and our old opponents the 42nd, coming out victorious on every occasion. While a match with the latter was in progress one afternoon, Fritz put three or four very large "shrap" over after a balloon which had its home not far from the camp. Pellets fell like hail all over the field, and large pieces made many regret that they had not their steel lids with them. How it is that no one was hit is a miracle. On voting-day several large Fritz bombing-planes were seen going toward our back areas, but they did not trouble us until their return journey, when they registered their " votes " with deadly effect. One hit the end of the Y.M.C.A. Hut, knocking it to pieces, and unfortunately wounding sixteen men. Bombs were also dropped on the main road, not far from the Palmer Baths, killing two outright. On account of low-hanging clouds it was practically impossible for the " Archies " to get the range of the invaders. It was on this day also that one of our little scouts brought down a huge Gotha near the Catacombs in full view of about one hundred of our fellows who were up there on a working-party. Thus, even " over here " voting-day was not without its disturbances.

During the period of our stay in Kortepyp, we were really in reserve to the Warneton sector, but as there was no necessity to move or help in any operations, it worried no one except the few who had to carry out reconnaissance. Our term in reserve finished, we moved camp again to Kemmel Shelters, where training on the same lines was resumed. This was at the beginning of December. It was on the 19th of the month that the battalion left Kemmel, just before mid-day, and very few, if any, could have felt regret, as that camp seemed to be a detached portion of the polar regions—bleak and miserable. Marching through mud and slush *via* Dranoutre and Neuve Eglise past the Palmer Baths and across the frontier into Belgium, we finally reached at about five o'clock a motley group of the ever-familiar, semi-circular huts, known as Waterlands Camp. This was what we were to call " home " for the next week or so. The camp was near Erquinghem and within a few minutes' walk of Nieppe, a town well remembered by all for the abundance of the standard meal—" Eggs and Chips."

The 42nd Battalion had taken over the line from near Tree Farm, south of Armentieres, to Burnt Farm, with the 44th in close support and the 43rd in support and ourselves in reserve.

Training was the order of the day while we were at this camp, but it was carried out under difficulties, for, owing to the wet weather, the ground had been churned up by countless thousands of feet. Consequently. when the heavy frost set in the ground was so uneven that drill was nearly out of the question. Working-parties to the lines were supplied from here, some being attached to the Engineers: the remainder of the battalion carried on with training. Christmas Day saw us practically where we had been the previous year, and as far as weather conditions go it was what we might call a real old-fashioned Christmas, such as is usually depicted on Christmas cards, heavy snow and a high wind blowing, but unfortunately we were not able to sit in front of the time-honoured log-fire. However, we had a dinner befitting the occasion to compensate for some of our discomforts. Large marquee tents were erected and fitted up with tables and forms, enabling the men to sit down in comparative comfort. Everything was of the best and in plenty—poultry, roast beef, plum pudding *ad lib*, and last, but not least, that glorious beverage of the bourgeois, BEER. One thing in particular that was appreciated by the " diggers " was the " slick " manner in which our officers played the role of waiters. A Pierrot show filled in the afternoon, and would have been still more enjoyable, if only we could have kept warm. On the 26th, owing to the 43rd Battalion relieving the 42nd, we had to move up into support at Erquinghem. From now until the end of the month the battalion was carrying on with nothing but working-parties. Who can forget them, the countryside icebound, the nights as dark as ink, and " umpteen " kilometres to the trenches, where we wired, cleared out trenches, made firesteps, and performed the general duties of " duckboard harriers." Then, on 3rd January of the New Year, we had the novel experience of a " tommy route-march," when the battalion embussed at Erquinghem shortly after breakfast, and moved back to the Kemmel Huts in the Locre area.

The old training routine was soon started again, and if it had not been for an old sand track, just below the camp, it is doubtful if much could have been done, as it was almost impossible to stand anywhere else. While here, the companies had to take turns in supplying working-parties of ninety men to repair roads and so forth—first of all out towards Messines, and later Neuve Eglise. We had a ride in motors on occasions, but not too often, good old " Shanks' pony " taking us many a weary kilometre in those days.

After the 21st, working-parties ceased, and training was once more resumed. It was at this time that the battalion had a revival of the fire-alarm stunt, everyone having to turn out at any hour of the night in fighting order. They were very successful as far as time went, and the rapidity with which we turned out evoked many compliments. Of course, no one was supposed to know when the alarm was to be sounded, but, strange to say, on those particular nights we always got fighting order ready before turning in, and—perhaps—taking our boots off. Hence our speed.

Preparations were now in progress for going into the line. Tin hats were re-covered and iron-rations, ammunition, and so forth were served out.

On the 28th we moved to Kortepyp, where we stayed the night, entraining on the light railway at 3 p.m. the following afternoon. Gum-boots were served out before we boarded the train. We travelled thus as far as Delennelle Farm, not far from Motor-car Corner. We followed the old trolley-track to the famous corner, and turned off to the left, wasting no time on the way, as everyone remembered Fritz's predilection for that spot. We continued on towards Surrey Farm. As we were going in, the enemy shelled Motor-car Corner heavily, but the battalion got through without any casualties. The machine gunners were, however, less fortunate, eleven of them being hit. "C" Company took over the left sector from just behind White Farm down to View Lane, "D" Company being in support to them. On the right "A" Company had from View Lane to Tool House, "B" Company occupying supports at Lys Farm.

This sector was considered a "home away from home," for although it was certainly wet and muddy, our days were now fairly free from that "screech and plonk" business. Many a little episode must come to memory at mention of Surrey Farm, Despierre Farm, Twenty-one Trees, Estaminet House, Pond House, View Lane, and Tool House.

The greater part of "No Man's Land" lay between our front line and the River Lys—the remainder on the opposite bank; so that it became necessary to establish outposts at different points along the river for the purpose of keeping watch against surprise. The river proved a very effective barrier, however, and rendered the chances of our being raided almost nil. When we first came in, the river and adjacent low-lying country were flooded, but nevertheless strong patrols, led by battalion scouts, went out each night to ensure our complete possession of "No Man's Land." Right along the bank of the Lys they would go, carefully stealing along, stopping and listening at times, and rarely if ever coming back without some information. Perhaps it would be an enemy working-party at the Laundry or machine guns firing from the Dyeworks or Soaphouse, and of those who were on those patrols, who has not assumed the prone as those machine guns at the Arches let drive? Besides the patrols and Lewis gun crews, everyone had something to do; if it was not ration-carrying, there was always trenches to repair, either to revet or to drain.

On the night of the 5th-6th we were relieved by the 43rd and moved back to Le Rossignol Camp, near Nieppe, without suffering a casualty *en route*.

The following eight days constituted what is known in the Army as a "spell." No one knows who first used that word in this sense, but all feel that his knowledge of English was scanty. The first day was devoted to a general cleaning up, a good bath and change of underwear being obtained at the baths at Nieppe. The inevitable working-parties for the trenches were supplied next day, and were of the never-to-be-forgotten type. Starting out at about three o'clock in the afternoon, we had to march through Romarin and the village of Ploegsteert, along the edge of the wood of that name, and then the fun used to start. Here began duckboards by the mile, holes by the thousand, and water deep enough to drown a man. A new support-line was in course of construction, and duckboards and revetting-frames had to be carried from the corner of Ploegsteert Wood along three kilometres of broken duckboards. It was, "Look out for the hole!" "Where is it?" "What the ——— did you say it was to the right for?" And so on, from start to finish. But it didn't matter, for if one missed one hole one was sure to find the next, so one might as well get wet first as last. The march home tried the best of the troops, their sodden boots and the long rough road making the feet very sore. It was generally two o'clock in the morning when we reached Le Rossignol, almost too weary to make our beds. But still, it was "all in a good cause"; a nip of S.R.D. and a good meal made the world look rosier, and then we would turn in and sleep till ten o'clock the next day. These parties were supplied daily during the eight days that we were at Le Rossignol, and to most of us it was a relief to go back to the peaceful trenches.

Our relief of the 43rd was quieter than the previous occasion of taking over. We held the same sector as before, except that "D" Company took the left sector, "B" Company the right, while "A" Company was in support to "D" Company, and "C" Company to "B" Company.

Patrolling was again the chief feature. "No Man's Land" had to be held, on account of the many outposts we established there. It was during this period that a somewhat sensational and wholly unauthorised raid was organised by four N.C.O.'s. They were going to cross by the wooden bridge just below "White Farm" outpost—take Lille, some say. As a matter of fact they got across, but were so quick returning that some of them fell into the Lys, and afterwards developed "P.U.O." The result was that Fritz destroyed part of the bridge later that night, and by so doing thwarted the purpose of the authorised raiders who went out the following night. Most will remember about this time "the dog" scare. A sentry on "D" Company Headquarters shot a large black dog, which was found on the following night dead out in "No Man's Land." It had a message-case and identity disc attached to its collar. The message was not very important; still, the result was that all stray dogs got a lively reception from this time forth.

Not many hours before our relief, a shell fell in "D" Company's cookhouse, killing two and wounding three—evidently retaliation for the shelling of one of the Boche cookhouses the previous afternoon. The Boche's great habit of shelling certain points at fixed times was very noticeable with regard to Despierre Farm, Battalion Headquarters. One could set one's watch to 9 a.m. whenever he started in the morning on this "possie." One morning he inflicted three casualties, wounding two and killing the Headquarters' Signaller-Sergeant. After eight days in this sector we were back again at Le Rossignol Camp, the 43rd having relieved us. The following Sunday, church parade was held at the White Chateau, in Nieppe, at which General Birdwood made a presentation of medals. During the training, which occupied our mornings, musketry was given a prominent place in the syllabus, the experiences at Cambrai being cited to show the troops what a rifle could do. On the night of the 1st of March we relieved the 43rd Battalion in the line at Le Bizet for the third time. The support-companies of the 43rd remained in the support lines, as our support-companies were engaged in carrying up gas cylinders to the front line in preparation for a gas attack. The Lys River having regained its normal level, we were enabled to occupy outposts which previously had been in too flooded a state to be approached.

Pond House, Estaminet House, Crown Prince Farm, and White Farm will hardly be forgotten by the scouts and the patrols of company men who nightly went the rounds of these outposts. Twice the imaginations of patrols worked overtime, but on investigating the posts whence the noises issued, they were able to laugh at their fears on finding one of the authors of the strange noises a working-party cleaning up an outpost and the others a pair of quarrelsome cats. "No Man's Land," patrols will tell you, is a region very far removed from the homely trench, and peopled with an infinite number of shades and fears—not at all the desolate, uninhabited place it seems from the front-line trench. We had to stay in only four days this time, which was just as well, as no blankets were carried. Fritz paid us marked attention with Minenwerfers the last two days, but we suffered no casualties, although a "medium" fell right in "Kiwi Street" just past the Light Railway line.

The 2nd Division relieved us on the night 4th-5th. This time we caught the light tramway cars at the big dump not far from Motor-car Corner. Very few knew exactly where we were going and just trusted to the train to stop at the right place. Evidently the engine-driver did not know either where to pull up, for we toured the tramway system until three in the morning, passing once right through the very camp which we were supposed to occupy. However, the train, or the driver, it has not been settled which, getting tired, we finally got off not too far from the camp at Le Romarin, our destination.

The next morning we rose early to prepare for our journey to the back areas for a "Dinkum" spell. All were in a good humour and nothing appeared to worry them. It was a glorious day with brilliant sunshine, the roads were in good order, and there was just a tinge of frost in the air. We marched with song and whistle as far as a paddock adjoining the railway station at Steenwerck, where we halted for lunch. At midday we entrained. It was a happy journey, even though we were packed together in the usual manner. *En route* we passed through Bailleul, Hazebrouck, Ebblinghem, St. Omer, and Wizernes, and just after dark we reached Lottinghem, where the battalion detrained, and after a cup of hot cocoa at the Y.M.C.A. marched to billets at Ques Ques and Verval.

PHASE VI.

CHAPTER 1.

Competitions and Sports at Ques Ques.—Disquieting Rumours.—Marching Orders.—Journey to the Somme to Check the German Advance.—Doullens and the Refugees.—The Crowded Road.—Some Expressions and Anecdotes.—Heilly and Franvillers.—Dug in near Vaux-sur-Somme.

Ques Ques will be remembered by the majority of the 41st Battalion, not so much as a particular village in France, but as the scene of one of those periodical spells out of the line, when training and sports went hand in hand, and everything was made a matter of competition. There were competitions in musketry, Lewis gun work, clean billets and cookers. Spring arrived early this year, and the weather was beautiful, allowing us to carry out a fine sports programme. The inter-company football matches caused keen rivalry. Two companies billeted on the hill at Verval were known as the "Highlanders," the other two with Headquarters down in the valley being called the "Lowlanders." In an exciting match between the two parties the "Lowlanders" came off victorious. Everyone displayed the greatest interest in the shooting competitions, and a vast improvement was soon noticeable, men acquiring far more confidence in themselves. There was a competition on the 19th March to decide the best platoon in the battalion, which resulted in a win for No. 9 Platoon, which was then under the command of Lieutenant Boyce "M.C." Two days later there was a lecture and gas demonstration at Harlette by the Divisional Gas Officer. In this way, life was made more interesting, and everyone was kept fairly busy carrying-on with these various shows. And then amid these pleasant surroundings came disquieting rumours, and we were ordered to prepare for a speedy move. Whither, no one could tell. Fritz's great push for Amiens was in full swing, but we knew little or nothing about it, and, when we moved to Eccke, we little thought that there would be practically no rest for us until we reached the Somme. The battalion entrained at Lottinghem together with the rest of the 11th Brigade, reaching Caestre at 5 p.m. on the 22nd. The billets at Eccke were scattered about all over the place, and were not very good. The following day there was a conference of C.O.'s at Brigade, and word came through that, owing to the serious situation down south, an immediate move would have to be made in the morning. To expedite the advance, all spare luggage and one spare blanket per man were stored here. Now commenced the historic dash of the Australian 3rd Division to the Somme, to stay the German push, which looked like swamping

Amiens unless an immediate stand was made. North of Eccke the long line of motor-buses was waiting, aboard which we squeezed, travelling thus as far as Ebblinghem. Something rather novel at that time to see a bus full of Aussies! After a picnic lunch on the grassy fields under a glorious blue sky we continued our journey to Blaringhem, where we had a night's rest. The following evening saw us again on the move, keeping close to the canal bank, making for Arques, where we entrained for Doullens. We had some time to wait for the train at Arques, and the cramped state of the trucks was not too pleasant, so that we were rather tired on reaching Doullens, and glad to get out to stretch our legs. We moved up to the Citadelle for lunch and a rest. A few showers worried us at times, but in the intervals the sun shone brightly, while the band played us martial airs and some of the old well-known tunes. After we had detrained at Doullens a few may remember encountering an individual, weighed down by his responsibilities and his fears, who, with flourishing Webley, controlled the traffic at the station crossing. As our column passed through, the traffic-control " bird " was the subject of chaff from all the diggers. A remark from one, laden down with his Lewis gun, drew a good laugh from his cobbers: " Say, Digger, don't let her off, or you'll get shell-shock."

It was at Doullens that we first realised the grave danger menacing the country-folk of this part of France. The fear of the Hun invasion was plainly stamped on the features of the people. All down the road from here onwards was a motley crowd of refugees of all ages, especially noticeable being the women-folk, young and old, dressed in their Sunday black, carrying bundles with all their valuables and personal belongings. Those who had too much to carry were pushing along the typical wide barrows, laden with household goods, linen, and utensils; others had handcarts. As they toiled along, they seemed weighed down with anxiety, and looked as though they hardly dared glance back, for fear they should see the hated Boche appearing over the horizon. It was a lamentable sight—this flight of a whole civilian population before the invading hordes. As far as the eye could see down the long wide road was a mighty stream of traffic, wagons and carts piled high with furniture, a strange medley of bedding, washstands, picture-frames, brooms, and saucepans, all thrown on in any fashion, testifying to the haste of departure. Amongst the panic-stricken men and women were dogs, goats, and cows, dogs often helping to drag the handcarts, and cows being driven along singly by old women or boys—the French peasant's inevitable family cow. Some of the people as they passed us could not even force a smile, so sure it seemed to them that all was over; indeed for most of them this great push meant the complete smashing-up of home and farm. The Hun would have to be driven back eventually somehow, and the only way would be to rally as quickly as possible and bring up guns and yet more guns, and shell him out of the towns and villages he had plundered. And so it was "good-bye homestead" to many thousands. They would return one day to find a ruin, a fragment of wall still standing perhaps, or in many cases no trace of dwelling at all. Is it any wonder that these poor village people should lose heart and give way to almost speechless despair, muttering "no bonne, no bonne," as they hurried by, instead of a cheery "bon jour" to one and all?

As the motor-lorries rumbled by, towing the big guns back to safety, gangs of Tommies accompanying them would stare in amazement at the sight of troops marching in a solid and orderly fashion actually towards the very source of that great Fear which had set them on the run, and some would vary their "Hy, lookout, Jerry's coming!" with sarcastic comments such as "You're going the wrong way, Digger—Jerry'll souvenir you and your ——— band too." One of the most remarkable features of our journey southwards was the new morale that the sight of our men instilled into the people. Company after company of sunburnt Australians marching by at ease, observing the usual march-discipline, but laughing and joking all the while, could not help striking these people as not only bizarre, but as an earnest of ultimate victory, even in this darkest hour. Weeping women had to restrain their tears as to their lips sprang automatically a "Vive l'Australie." All this mass of traffic was pouring in one direction, only the Aussies were hastening towards the line, our own 3rd Division on the long trail of the Somme to save Amiens and stem the great German thrust towards the coast. It is not for this history to criticise the big retreat that March. All that need be said is that, whatever was the cause, and whoever was to blame, the troops concerned had some very unpleasant things said about them.

The 3rd Division had now been transferred to the 10th Corps, 3rd Army. Our battalion was ordered to billet at Authie, but owing to the places being heavily shelled, a new order was issued, making the 41st an outpost battalion, with Headquarters at Authieule. This was done owing to the obscurity of the whole situation, it being feared that the Germans had broken through with armoured cars and cavalry. At 5.30 p.m., after an hour and a-half's march, we reached Authieule, and our main line of resistance was immediately selected. Later, word came through that we were to billet there, and that the men were to get as much rest as possible. Considering that we had scarcely enjoyed a wink of sleep since leaving Eecke, the general satisfaction at the issue of this order can well be imagined. But there is many a slip ———; the situation was too critical to allow time to sleep.

At 11 p.m. an urgent movement message was received, and at midnight the battalion set out again on its weary march, making for Thievres, *via* Amplier and Orville, a distance of about ten miles. Fortunately, we did not have to march all the way to the Somme, as here again we boarded the buses, which took us to Franvillers. What a journey; in the darkness of the early hours of the morning of the 27th, jolting along southwards to an unknown destination! A short march brought the battalion to the outskirts of Heilly, where a halt was made for breakfast. Here a few were able to snatch a few moments' sleep, pillowing their heads on their packs, which were soon after to be put away in the store, as the battalion had now to "gird its armour on"—that is, get into fighting order. It was here that we first came within reach of Fritz, whose long-range "rubber guns" sent over some "toute-de-suiters," which landed close to the marching column. They only served to quicken up our pace towards the source of trouble. The task allotted our Brigade was really colossal. The four battalions had to hold a Divisional front which ran from the Ancre in the north to the Somme in the south. The country consisted of high plateaux under cultivation and valleys studded with dense wood. It was a wedge-shaped strip of ground that we had to hold, with the old town of Corbie, whose twin towers rose high above the surrounding landscape, standing at the apex of the "V." From Corbie the wedge widened out towards the east, and incidentally towards the enemy. At this period, the position was vitally important. Here was one of the keys to Amiens, and at all costs it had to be defended against every assault. Such was our task, and well may we be proud that we, a mere handful of Australians, were thought worthy of holding the broad stretch of downland between the two rivers, and that we triumphantly stayed the enemy, baulking him just at the moment when he thought Amiens was at last in his grasp.

The line we had to occupy extended from Mericourt-L'Abbe to Sailly-le-Sec. Remains of a British Division were to reinforce us, but their morale was practically broken, and so they were sent out to reorganise, and the only troops available to assist in the defence consisted of a gallant brigade of cavalry, which withdrew, and covered our right flank south of the Somme, on the first night of our arrival. Thus it will be clearly seen that the brunt of the whole attack would fall on us, or at any rate upon our brigade. And we were ready for any emergency, moving forward carefully, feeling our way towards the enemy. We could not tell how soon we might be on to him; at any moment, perhaps over the next rise, the whiz, whiz, of his machine gun bullets might greet us. This was real open warfare, fraught with novelty and excitement. Never before had we experienced anything like this. All we knew for certain was that Fritz was lying in readiness somewhere ahead. Only a few shells were coming over, and our casualties were light during our approach march, for we avoided all roads and tracks. On the way we crossed mined bridges, where the sentries, knowing full well the importance of their job, were ever on the alert, ready at a moment's notice to ignite the fuse and send the bridge "sky high." Advancing thus, we eventually reached the ridge which it had been decided to hold. The battalion positions between the Ancre River and the Bray-Corbie road were the 43rd and part of the 41st, with later the 44th; from the road to the Somme there was the 42nd with the 41st in support. Our frontage of about a mile was in the vicinity of Vaux-sur-Somme, in which "D" Company, detailed for duty work, took up its headquarters. The artillery, which later was to line the hills and woods from Franvillers to Corbie and beyond, had not yet got into position, the only battery present being "Y" Battery of 13-pounders, which was indulging in some fine "pot-shots" from a camouflaged position north of Bray Road. Our line was soon strongly established in the positions mentioned above, thus checking for all time the Germans' westward push. From now on, the offensive gradually passed into our hands, ending, as everyone knows, in that great victorious advance from Corbie to the Hindenburg Line, and beyond. It was just after we arrived at Vaux-sur-Somme that a Tommy, displaying the running ribbon on his chest, was accosted by a digger with "What did you get that ribbon for, chum?" "Why, choom, I got it for the retreat at Mons." "Well," said the digger, with Australian forcefulness, "I suppose you will be wanting a ————— bar for this show."

The Australian has a great admiration for the Scotch. There is an incident related by a member of a labour corps, a Scotchman by birth, which illustrates this friendly feeling between the Diggers and the Jocks. It happened at Franvillers during our early days on the Somme. The Scot told the tale as follows:—"I was guarding my dump, when two Australians, not fou', but vera careful," came along. Taking no notice of me, one of them said, "Digger, this ————— barbed wire will just do us." I said, "But that is my barbed wire." "Oh," retorted the colonial, "and what the ————— has it got to do with you, and who the h—— are you, anyhow?" I said "I belong to the —th labour company; I am from the ——th Highland Regiment." "Shake hands, Jock," they both cried immediately, and they solemnly shook hands, and one presented me with a bottle of champagne from the inside of his shirt, and then, with a "So long! Digger," they both left the dump.

On The Way To The Somme — March 1918.

PHASE VII.

CHAPTER I.

On the Somme.—Our Dispositions.—Hun's Fruitless Attacks.—The Loss of Hamel by the British.—Our Successful Raids at Sailly-le-Sec.—Aeroplane Activity.—Baron Richthofen's Death.—Heavy Bombardment of our Sector.—The "Retreat from Bonnay."

The preceding chapter has described the arrival of the 41st Battalion on the Somme, and it would seem appropriate at this point in the narrative to digress for a moment to consider one or two aspects of the situation.

Previous to this, the 3rd Division had felt a little out of the picture, when men of the other divisions used to hold forth about the Somme, recounting their exploits in the famous stunts of 1916. There was often a good deal of heated arguing, which sometimes ended in a bit of a " stoush " when " eggs-a-cooked " met a party of the " Diamond " or " Circular " Divisions, who started " skiting " about Bullecourt, or comparing the mud and hardships of that first severe winter with what we had to put up with at Messines and Flanders.

Now no longer would the Somme be thrown up against us in this way—" We came, we saw, we conquered."

Arriving on the scene, as we did, in the early days of a particularly fine spring, we found the country at its very best, and instead of the mud-bound waste most of us had imagined, we discovered a beautiful land of hills and vales, bright with flowers, with the sinuous Somme and its lagoons as the central feature.

There was dust—plenty of it; white, chalky dust—but no mud that summer, and even when we had advanced into the region of the old battlefields, the ground was hard and dry, and the shell-holes all overgrown with grass and weeds. But " revenons a nos moutons," we left the battalion dug in near Vaux-sur-Somme, as reserve to the Brigade.

The 10th Brigade arrived on the 28th March and took over the line from the River Ancre to the Bray-Corbie Road. The 42nd Battalion closed in to its right, the dispositions then being from right to left between the Somme and Bray-Corbie Road : 42nd with 44th in support, and 43rd with 41st in support. The right flank of the 42nd and 41st Battalions was refused along the Somme from Bouzencourt, as the disposition and strength of the English troops on the opposite bank had not been definitely ascertained, and British cavalry was still patrolling in the vicinity of Hamel. The night previous the cavalry had advanced to Sailly Laurette, and cleared a small enemy advance guard out of the town, taking prisoners and machine guns.

And so we waited for the great German avalanche, that appeared to have got hung up somewhere. Later we heard that his men and horses were very fatigued by the time they reached our positions, the constant pushing on, sleeping in the rain without sufficient shelter, and lack of hot meals, making a spell absolutely necessary for the men. They also needed some reorganization, for many had been left behind engaged in looting, and most of them, officers included, were in all stages of intoxication, and consequently a little perplexed as to their whereabouts. Evidence of this was not lacking. In our own sector several Boches strayed into our lines, and reports from the adjoining units show that there, also, the enemy lost several men in a similar manner. One of these, mounted on a motor-cycle, was caught passing through our lines, apparently bound for Amiens. Enemy light artillery 105 and 77 mm. guns kept up well with the advance, and shelled roads and gullies at intervals.

It was not until some days later that we obtained efficient artillery support. On the 29th, our divisional artillery put in an appearance, greatly to our relief.

By the 30th the enemy directly opposite in the Somme Valley—about a divisional front—were relieved by fresher men; the number of his guns had increased, and they were well supplied with shells. By now the Boche was fully aware that his march on Amiens was to be blocked. He had seen us " dug in " and had suffered casualties when we advanced to a suitable " digging-in " position, after getting in touch. One of the prisoners stated that his mates believed the way to be barred by Scotchmen.

At midday on the 30th March his barrage of heavy and light artillery and machine-gun fire dropped on our front between the Bray-Corbie Road and the Bois de Hamel—about three kilometres wide—and shortly after, his infantry advanced in three solid waves. All caution forgotten, they came on in the old massed formation, probably hoping that numbers would " put the wind up " the troops who had dared to make a stand. He did not reckon on " Aussies," however, and the waves wilted before a well-sustained and murderous fire from machine guns and rifles before they had got within 800 yards of our outpost line. As far as our battalion was concerned, " B " Company, which occupied the outpost or picket line, was responsible for checking the advance. Our men shot coolly and with great accuracy, until ammunition had almost run out, and they were obliged to send back an urgent request for more, which the 43rd supplied.

Other units on our flanks put up good work with similar success. Two hours later another attack was launched, but having in mind the disaster that befell the first, the enemy advanced on more open order. This attack was more fruitless than the first, and he was compelled to " dig in " where it broke down. Communications with units adjacent to us were quickly established and all was reported " O.K." A word of praise is due to the 3rd Divisional Artillery, which under fire from enemy " heavies " toiled with the greatest skill and gallantry. The " Diggers " all expressed great admiration at the way they handled their teams, which was thoroughly Australian.

While speaking of the artillery, one cannot pass on without recording the famous entry of one of our batteries which had been *en route* and came into action during the attack. Picture galloping gun-teams such as are seen in manœuvres crossing open fields, down gullies and up the other side, then add an enemy barrage with shells falling all round causing casualties, but not checking their mad gallop, and you have an impression of what the infantry saw when this battery galloped up and unlimbered near Welcome Wood on the crest of the rise and through open sights fired into the masses of approaching Germans. Deeds such as these, though unsung, did much to bring the Australian Corps into that happy state of mutual confidence that was responsible for their overwhelming victories later in the year.

Our casualties were light, being well under thirty, while the losses inflicted on the enemy were to be estimated in hundreds. Hun stretcher-bearers toiled late into the night, removing dead and wounded. No. 6 Platoon, " B " Company, claimed the biggest bag for the day. The end of March found us well established, the increase in our artillery support and the presence of fresh troops discouraging further enemy attempts to continue the thrust for Amiens along the Somme Valley. We had expected a more determined effort to break our resistance, and the results of well-sustained rapid fire put all in better spirits. Self-confidence never wavered, though the weather was showery, and to those in the trenches sleep would come only with utter fatigue. Travelling kitchens were brought well forward, and for a while stayed near B.H.Q., providing hot meals as often as possible. Also once more, as formerly, the good old S.R.D. scored a great triumph over cold tea. The battalion canteen occupied a dugout near B.H.Q., and, although it was hard to obtain supplies, tobacco and cigarettes were plentiful, and found a ready sale in the line.

During a patrol, identification was obtained from a Boche killed on the 30th. From him it was found that the Hun regiment opposite to us, when we first reached the Somme area, was the 31st R.I.R., 18th Division. This regiment was relieved on the 1st April, and on the 2nd the first battery of enemy foot-artillery (155 mm.) moved in to support the infantry. At dusk the observer of this battery, a lance-corporal, set out with telephone and gear to find an O.P. and wandered into our lines. He was wounded and brought to our R.A.P. for treatment, giving good information later. While in the front line astride the Bray-Corbie road, a sentry was on duty one night as a " weary willie " whined overhead, and remarked to his mate, " Gee ! Bill, that fellow is going a long way." " Yes," remarked his mate immediately, " I guess it will reach the Tommy front line " !

On the 4th April, after artillery preparation the previous day that put us on the " qui vive," the 16th British Division was driven out of its position before Hamel and the woods on the higher ground to the south. We were continually subjected to enemy practice-barrages, but as a rule very few casualties resulted, the range being incorrect, and visibility too poor to obtain correction. After his capture of Hamel and the woods above, our artillery kept up a harassing fire on the newly-captured territory, and his casualties must have been severe.

The weather soon began to improve, and 'planes of both sides came out to take every advantage of the opportunity for making photos and exercising their machine guns. It was rather a rare sight sight to see Boche 'planes well over our lines. Our anti-aircraft machine guns had won much respect from his airmen, and they were generally wary of drawing our fire. Those who did not penetrate any distance flew out of range of even " Archie " fire, but such 'planes were engaged in photographing our back areas, at which art the Boche had the advantage of our airmen, who were compelled to photograph at lower altitudes. However, the greater risk of drawing all kinds of fire was cheerfully undertaken by our pilots. We witnessed several strenuous air-battles, in which enemy 'planes invariably had the preponderance numerically. Seven 'planes " crashed " the first clear day, but as they fell far behind Fritz's lines, we could not determine their nationality. It was one day, when four of our 'planes were cruising about overhead, that a Hun airman piloting a British machine swooped down out of the sky. Before he made off he just dropped a souvenir. One of our Headquarter's signallers happened to catch sight of the falling object, and supposing it to be a message-bag thrown from one of our planes, climbed out of the trench and ran up the hill towards the spot where he expected it to land. Fortunately the " message " fell about two hundred yards over the ridge in front of him. There was an explosion, of course, but our eager little " sig." did not associate it with the message, which he meant to souvenir at all costs. Seeing a man of another battalion hurrying along ahead of him, he shouted, " Hey ! did you see a message-bag drop over there ? " " Message-bag be ———d ! " came the breathless reply, " that was a ——————— bomb ! "

Visibility being excellent, battalion observers were able to find targets for the artillery; and enemy transport, and in fact all movement on Fritz's part, received plenty of attention. Retaliation for this in the form of harassing fire was directed to all gullies and woods affording likely cover for troops, but our casualties were slight. On the 10th April the villages of Sailly-le-Sec, Vaire-sous-Corbie, and Vaux-sur-Somme were heavily shelled, but beyond reducing many more houses to ruins, no casualties occurred, as no troops were stationed in the villages.

Baths were opened at Bonnay, and we were able to enjoy a much-needed wash and change, whenever it was necessary, bath-parades taking place during lulls in the enemy's " strafes."

At night our 'planes were noticed to be unusually active bombing the enemy back areas.

During the night 13th-14th the relief of the 43rd Battalion was carried out by us without casualties. Our patrols from the first had kept " No Man's Land " clear, and this night a reconnaissance of the enemy's outpost line was made with a view to the possibilities of a raid. The following night marked the beginning of a series of successful raids, which eventually compelled the enemy to withdraw all outposts, and leave us in undisputed possession of " No Man's Land." The 1st Australian Division, in the North of France, was also practising similar tactics, and the German High Command found it necessary to issue special warning to troops opposing Australians, whose skill at this game they freely recognised. Almost every twenty-four hours Division required identifications, and it is satisfactory to be able to record that they were never disappointed. We were fortunate in having several fine scouts in the battalion, and to these and the officers who so skilfully handled the patrols in their charge the highest praise is due. Better work of this nature, with fewer casualties attendant, has certainly never been done before or since in the whole history of the War by any other battalion.

The first raid was carried out by a patrol of sixteen men and two Headquarters' scouts, under the command of 2nd Lieutenant F. J. Burtenshaw. A machine-gun outpost was rushed, the gunner leaving his post to meet the supposed relief, thus making the task easier. Two Boches were killed and three taken prisoners, among the latter the sergeant in charge of the post. For this fine example of personal bravery and prompt action Lieutenant Burtenshaw was awarded the Military Cross. On this occasion one of the scouts, who spoke German, discovered from the German sergeant that he had just been about to open a home parcel when surprised, and much disgust was expressed in the scout's dugout at missing a feed that would wash down beautifully with a nip of rum.

About this time Lieutenant T. R. O'Sullivan, a gallant and courteous officer, was killed, while asleep in his dugout. He lies in the little cemetery at Bonnay, and, together with so many more brave men, whose bones strew the way to victory, he has earned the true glory that lies in sacrifice. May we never forget such men!

The night of the 15th-16th April saw Lieutenant Tredenick leading a party against a Boche post just south of the Bray-Corbie Road. In spite of pluckily cutting the wire and tackling the post although discovered, they were unable to get a live Boche, but left two dead ones behind them. Lance-corporal Croft, a scout, who was wounded, and gallantly guided the party safely back, deserves great praise.

On the 18th April a patrol under Lieutenant C. H. Butler, M.C., accompanied by Headquarters' Scouts Dixon and Murray, rushed a hostile post under heavy rifle and machine-gun fire, and secured two prisoners, killing nine. No casualties were sustained by our patrol. The Divisional Commander congratulated those concerned on their really fine exploit.

Five Boches were killed during a raid on the following morning at 3.30, and identification secured. Our casualties were again nil, although the hostile post offered strong resistance.

Again, on the 20th a patrol under Lieutenants Wiles and Burtenshaw was successful in capturing a prisoner. Credit for this is mainly due to Lieutenant Wiles, who chased the Hun almost into an occupied post, closed with him, and dragged him back to the patrol. For this he received a D.S.O. Our casualties were one stretcher case and one slightly wounded, stick bombs being the cause. Machine-gun fire from the enemy was very heavy, but did no damage, although the night was very bright. Thus the total results of the raids carried out up to the 20th of April were:—Prisoners, six; killed, twenty-one; costing us in wounded nine cases, only two of which had to be evacuated.

As the work of developing the trench-systems went on, artillery on both sides fired on all targets presenting themselves, whenever visibility permitted observation, though the enemy artillery relied mostly on harassing fire, "shooting-up" gullies and woods where the presence of our troops was suspected. Reliefs with the 43rd were carried out every six days. In all our stay on the Somme, aerial activity was never so marked as on the 21st of April, when Captain Baron von Richthofen, the famous

Raiding Hun Post – Sailly-le-Sec – 1918

German airman, introduced his "Circus" to us. This "Circus" then consisted of six red triplanes, each supposed to have accounted for twenty-one Allied 'planes, and piloted by "aces." Luckily our 'planes were out in force, and before the close of the day four of the "Circus" had crashed. The Baron, flying very low, pursued one of our R.E. 8's which had got into trouble, and came within range of a nest of anti-aircraft machine guns, when about two kilometres over our lines. A machine gunner of the 53rd A.F.A. was credited with bringing him down. The enemy immediately shelled the fallen plane, and continued to do so throughout the night. However, that did not deter souvenir-hunters from making a haul, and it was hardly a whole machine that was salvaged by the R.F.C. The owners of bits of the 'plane are legion. In fact, there must be as many relics of it as there are of the True Cross. Next day three more of Fritz's airmen lost the number of their mess. At 3.30 a.m. on the 24th, the enemy opened up an intense bombardment of all gullies, particularly that in which the battalion was situated. The bombardment lasted five hours without slackening, after which, till late in the day, he continued dropping "hate" at short intervals. The greater percentage of these were gas shells, but, thanks to the excellent gas discipline, only two or three men were evacuated gassed. Our front and picket lines did not receive much attention, and communications both with them and neighbouring battalions were maintained. The shelling was merely a diversion to cover an attack *en masse* on Villers Bretonneux, south of the Somme. Two small attacks made on the 29th Battalion, A.I.F., which held the line near the canal, were repulsed with heavy loss to the enemy, entirely without artillery support. It is estimated that during the first five hours over four thousand shells fell in our vicinity. Our "echelon" party at Bonnay was forced to take cover in trenches near the town, an action which will long be remembered by the battalion as the famous "Retreat from Bonnay."

CHAPTER 2.

The Last Raids at Sailly-le-Sec.—German Prisoners and their Opinions.—Diggers and Dugouts.—The Spell at Franvillers.—The "Toute-de-Suiters."—Billets at Pont Noyelles and Sports.—Presentation of Medals at Allonville by General Sir W. R. Birdwood.—Anniversary Dinner at Querrieu Chateau.—Celebrating the Battalion's Departure from Queensland.—Sir D. Haig's Inspection.—The Move up to Villers-Bretonneux.

Our last successful raid, which earned the "M.C." for the officer in charge, was carried out by 2nd Lieutenant S. L. Robinson, who, after preliminary reconnaissance, rushed a post and captured a prisoner. On this occasion the patrol had artillery support, this probably putting the enemy machine gunners on the alert, as we sustained casualties—one killed and two wounded.

Three further attempts to raid enemy posts were fruitless, the Boche being by that time so " windy " that on approach of our fighting patrols he invariably withdrew without offering resistance to his front line, where barbed wire prevented our following him.

Towards the end of the month our trench-mortars were busy, shelling enemy positions and assisting the artillery in affording covering fire during raids.

The 34th Battalion relieved us on the night of May 1st-2nd.

The month of April was a most important one in the battalion's history. Till relief, we had held the line continually for thirty-six days—a record; the longest period up to then being nineteen days. During that time the amount of work done by the battalion in constructing a defensive system was astonishing. In this work the old French trench-system was utilised as far as possible. A very satisfactory amount of salvage was collected, besides over one hundred articles for the Australian War Muesum, many of these being of historic value, mementoes of minor enterprises or unsuccessful Boche attacks.

The R.M.O., Captain E. S. Meyers, did splendid work under most trying circumstances, often dressing cases under heavy shell fire. Indeed he appeared to be indefatigable. By " carrying-on " so gallantly he has earned the sincerest admiration of all ranks.

It is interesting to note the opinions of the prisoners captured during our stay here. Most of them were certain that there were at least four times as many Australians on the front as were actually there, as wherever they were sent they seemed always to strike Australians. When told that there were thousands of Americans already fighting, and hundreds of thousands actually training in France, they seemed to think that the chances of their country winning the War were rather slight. These men were very profuse in their assurances that they admired the " Aussies " very much, and did not cherish any hatred towards them. Asked when the War would finish, most were of the opinion that it would not last till Christmas, lack of enemy man-power being the main cause, while other factors were shortages of food, necessities, and equipment, due to our blockade.

It is certain that the enemy push would never have reached Amiens to schedule-time if the enemy's troops had had to depend on their own food supply alone. As it was, much of their food was looted from captured territory.

If ever one is asked to explain why the Aussie soldier is called a " digger," one need only recall the burrowing we did at the Somme to supply a plausible answer. Both reserve lines were in deep re-entrants, and in the bottom of each, on the side nearest the enemy, all the most suitable ground was occupied by dugouts, the sloping banks being full of them. As a rule, when the gullies were shelled, the greater part of the shells fell across on the other side. Towards the end of our stay in the sector, the engineers constructed deep, comfortable dugouts in Shrapnel Gully (the forward Headquarters gully), and with the chalk from these built several traverses along the valley, a large camouflage screen of branches hiding the work from enemy cameras. The average digger's "possie" was dug well into a sloping bank, the roof being at the head from five to six feet high, and at the foot one to two feet. Ground-sheets were spread to run rain off, but many, preferring the sheets to keep damp out, made trips to the nearest village, where from the ruins they obtained corrugated iron enough to cover the "home," as well as straw for the "floor." The width of such a "possie" was usually three to four feet, but where men camped in pairs or threes the places were widened to suit. There was a certain amount of risk in leaving too much soil on top of a "possie," even if it was only a foot or so overlapping one's pillow. This left the sleepers liable to accident, and caused a few casualties.

The morning of the 2nd May saw the battalion moving out of its positions by companies, as relief by the 34th Battalion proceeded. Guides were posted at crossroads, and these picked up the platoons in column and took them to Heilly, where, on the green where we had breakfasted thirty-six days previously, a hot meal and a generous "nip" waited for all. Needless to say, the meal was much appreciated, for it was several hours past the usual mealtime when we reached the green. From there the battalion marched to Franvillers (three kilometres from Heilly), where we billeted.

Franvillers will hardly be held in affectionate remembrance by any 41st digger. It was overcrowded and badly drained, and the billets had fallen out of repair considerably. Still, it was better than the line.

Very little work was done for a day or two. The "Divvy Pierrots" gave an entertainment at La Houssoye, where they got "a good hearing." Bath-parades were held, the battalion being marched by platoons to the River Ancre, near Heilly, where underclothes were overhauled or changed. On the 4th, the 42nd Battalion held a sports meeting, which the 41st attended in force.

The battalion was now reorganised, and officers and scouts made reconnaissances of the positions we were to occupy in case of the enemy attempting to break through, when it would fall to our lot to counter-attack. The number of our guns was increasing daily, and they kept up a lively bombardment on enemy positions, this probably tending to upset any enemy preparations for continuing the offensive on that front. At Franvillers two rather ancient heavies were in action, the shells, as they left the gun, making a very "wobbly" sound. On the 6th, about 150 prisoners passed through the town; the result of a successful enterprise carried out by the 9th and 10th Brigades.

Beyond occasional bombing raids, when several bombs fell in our vicinity, we fancied there was nothing to fear from Fritz while in the "back area," but we were rudely disillusioned on the night of the 8th at nearly midnight, when an enemy naval gun (called by diggers "the india-rubber gun" or "toute-de-suiter") opened up on the town. Twenty shells dropped in the buildings, "getting" two Tommies, but causing no casualties in the battalion.

Pont Noyelles was the next town touched at by the "six-bob-a-day tourists." Billets resembled those of Franvillers. "A" and "C" Companies camped in tents outside the village west of L'Hallue River. There were plenty of fine pools in the vicinity of Pont Noyelles, and they were well frequented by swimmers, the water being quite warm after the spell of sunny weather.

Again, on the 11th sports were held near "A" Company's tents, rain and long-range shells spoiling things somewhat. Two enemy naval guns kept strafing at five-minute intervals for long periods each day, most of the shells falling just beyond Querrieu, a village one kilometre distant from Pont Noyelles. It was rumoured that Brigade Headquarters had the "wind up" badly, for several shells fell in the grounds of their chateau. The "toute-de-suite" shell has a very demoralising effect. Coming from many miles away, it drops from the sky like lightning, often arriving before the sound of the gun that fires it.

Medals and ribbons awarded to officers, N.C.O.'s, and men of the 3rd Australian Division were presented to them by General Sir W. R. Birdwood at Allonville. As was to be expected, after the strenuous time just gone through by the division, the number of recipients was large, being somewhere about two hundred. Amongst honours falling to the battalion, Lieutenant H. J. Wiles was awarded the D.S.O., Lieutenant C. H. Butler a bar to the M.C., and Private E. Dixon, M.M., Headquarters' scout, the D.C.M.

While returning from a reconnaisance of the Villers Bretonneux sector on the 15th, Lieutenant F. J. Burtenshaw, M.C., a very promising officer who had won much distinction during our stay in the line before Sailly-le-Sec was killed by a heavy shell. Lieutenant S. L. Robinson, who was with him, was slightly wounded. Lieutenant Burtenshaw was buried next day in the Querrieu cemetery by Chaplain Major Mills, M.C.

Illustrative of the strange incongruities of war, that evening a dinner in celebration of the date on which the battalion left Queensland was held in the Querrieu Chateau. Brigadier-General Cannan, C.B., and C.O's of sister battalions were present. The function passed off very pleasantly.

The 11th Brigade was inspected on the afternoon of the 17th by Sir Douglas Haig, and the appearance of all ranks drew favourable comment from the inspector.

Final sports for that period were held on the recreation ground near Querrieu. As with the previous meeting, rain interfered greatly with the proceedings, and several events, including the swimming programme, had to be cut out, much to the disgust of enthusiasts. At 6 p.m., 19th May, specialists set out by motor-lorry to relieve equal numbers of the 15th Battalion at Villers Bretonneux. The route taken was through the deserted city of Amiens and from thence to Villers Bretonneux along the main Amiens-St. Quentin Road. This is one of the finest roads in France. Wide, well-kept, with a fine avenue of large shady trees throughout its length, it runs due east and west in a straight line almost the whole way. Motorists amongst the specialists rhapsodised about it. It is, in fact, the track on which, in pre-war days, the Grand-Prix motor-race was annually run.

Relief of the 15th Battalion was completed without casualties to either battalion by the following midnight.

CHAPTER 3.

In Front of Villers Bretonneux.—Battalion Dispositions.—The International Post.—Zouaves.—The Gassing of "A" Company.—Blangy Tronville.—Beauties of the Somme in Summer.—Swimming.—The Last Five days in the Line at Villers Bretonneux.—Back to the Vicinity of Frechencourt.

Villers Bretonneux, apparently an up-to-date and prosperous town before the war, had been reduced to ruins since the Boche advance. It will be remembered by all "Aussie" troops that this town, a key position to Amiens, was recaptured from the enemy by the 13th and 15th Australian Brigades, one of the most brilliant feats figuring in Australian war history. The sorely-harassed staffs of the English Divisions backing up these brigades were very sceptical when the Aussie staffs made known their plans for the recapture, the chief feature of which was the surrounding of the town.

When we took over the Somme area, the twin towers of the church were still intact. On our arrival in the town we found the church totally demolished. From

Sailly-le-Sec we had seen dense red clouds, smoke and brick dust, floating away over Villers Bretonneux during bombardment by enemy "heavies," and so expected to see ruin, though sufficient remained to indicate that the town had once been a very fine one. Amongst many imposing buildings were five chateaux and two schools. Buildings affording the best view of the enemy lines, and having good cellars, were used as O.P.'s and Headquarters for trench-mortars and artillery.

Battalion Headquarters was situated in a chalk quarry a few hundred yards from the town, on the main Amiens Road, and close to a deep railway cutting. The dugouts in the quarry were up-to-date and dry, and afforded a delightfully cool retreat from the sun's glare and hostile "hate." Later, these were connected to the railway cutting by tunnel. The cutting was a fairly safe route to the front line, and the tunnel did away with much of the movement—unavoidable at any Headquarters—that was likely to draw attention from enemy 'planes and observation balloons. As an illustration of the necessity for taking all precautions to prevent the giving away of information to the enemy, and camouflaging positions, it was later found that on a captured enemy map dated May, 1918, every position we occupied was accurately shown. It is therefore small matter for wonder that Battalion Headquarters was shelled occasionally, though of course we had then no idea that Fritz was so well posted with information.

For the first time in the active career of the battalion we were in touch with the French and also the extreme right flank of the British Army. Runners will remember the "International Post" and lick their lips reflectively in memory of at least one bright spot in the dreary monotony of the War. When the advance party reached the sector, a runner was made acquainted with the International Post, and what he found there seemed to please him mightily, so that it was several days before his cobbers could "get the strength" of his volunteering to be the Aussie runner to stay on duty with the French. Perhaps when we say that the French do not as a rule drink tea, no further explanation is required.

Before long the town had been explored thoroughly by industrious "Diggers," and all the foodstuffs the enemy was unable to carry away during his occupation went to swell the rations. It was salvaged, too, at considerable risk, though when we had learnt the danger points it was not so bad, for Fritz was ever methodical in his shelling. All will remember the fine view we had through one of the railway bridges which made it necessary for one to exercise caution and nimbleness in dodging across the line above the station; also the unhealthy place in the vicinity of the station, where hundreds of tons of spirit and lubricant oil were destroyed by the retreating British.

The inevitable Brasserie—or rather its ruins—was probably the most visited place in the whole collection of interesting buildings. Naturally when one is on tour, one wishes to see as much as possible. A few of the "Diggers," however, will think of that brewery cellar with blushes. Some disappointed seeker after vin blanc had upended a dead Fritz at the bottom of the stairs. This ghastly and lifelike guard drove subsequent searchers away at the toute.

At the western side of the town, facing the enemy, deep, wide trenches had been dug as tank traps. On our taking over the sector, the trench-systems were greatly improved. "No Man's Land" was thickly covered with crops, and patrolling was difficult. At first we were impressed with the quietness of the sector. It was hard to determine the enemy's positions, for his movements were guarded. Our front line at one point lay in a hollow, and it was a common sight to see "Diggers" perched on the parapet overhauling their clothes. Observers of the 15th Battalion had seen enemy movement at Monument Wood, a small wood surrounding a farmhouse and occupying about three acres.

Our front line opposite this point ran past a café, across a road leading out past the farmhouse. A walk of eighty yards from our line along this road would take one into hostile territory. There was a derelict tank some distance from the point of Monument Wood furthest from this road. It was later shot up as a probable sniper's post. Out in the more open ground, in the vicinity of a ruined British aerodrome, and also to our right, opposite the French, where "No Man's Land" was wider, lay the remnants of several 'planes—Allied and Boche. It was possible to improve our trenches, for the crops concealed movement, and the enemy had no high vantage ground from which to observe our lines.

On the night 25th-26th May the town and supports were heavily strafed with gas shells of the mustard variety. The strafe lasted from 7.45 p.m. till midnight and from 3 till 5 a.m. The front line did not receive much, Fritz being afraid of gassing his own men, but "A" support company suffered severely, and notwithstanding that the company was moved to a fresh position next morning, the heavy concentration that clung to grass and crops affected the entire company so much that it was found necessary to evacuate everyone.

Airmen took advantage of the fine sunny weather, and daily entertained us with "dog fights." Several enemy 'planes were brought down during the period. An attack was expected on the 25th, but did not materialise. On the 27th and 28th, hostile shelling was far above normal, but we were fortunate in suffering no casualties during relief, which was completed by 2 a.m. on the 29th, the battalion moving back three kilometres along the Amiens road to White Chateau in the Bois L'Abbe. Headquarters and R.A.P. were in the chateau, and companies were established in neighbouring trenches, already dug. The remainder of the month passed uneventfully, shelling causing little discomfort, occurring mostly at night. The R.A.P. was the scene of considerable bustle daily. The majority of the cases paraded for sore eyes and throats, caused by mustard gas. A large percentege of these " gas " cases were unable to speak for several weeks. Much credit is due to these men for carrying on in spite of such a fine excuse for " swinging the lead," a practice which the Aussies, always thorough, have brought to the level of a fine art. Let it be hoped that this practice arises only from the appeal it makes to their artistic natures.

Two unsuccessful raids were made by the front line battalions of the Brigade while we were in support, and Fritz retaliated an hour later, carrying through a successful raid, but leaving a prisoner in our front line. From him normal identification was secured. A later attempt to raid our lines south of the railway line was repulsed, one dead and one wounded being left with us. In order to recuperate and get ready in case of an enemy advance, when we were to counter-attack, the battalion took up new positions three kilometres further to the rear, along the Somme, near Blangy-Tronville, our positions in Bois L'Abbe being taken over by the 39th Battalion of the 10th Brigade which relieved our brigade on the 4th.

During the whole period we were in Villers Bretonneux a unit of the R.A.S.C. under Captain Ingram, besides giving us much assistance by the loan of motor-lorries for transport, when we came out of the line, regaled us with excellent pierrot shows.

Although it was not yet time for us to get back to the " Bock " areas our stay at Blangy-Tronville was a fair spell. Summer being by then well on the way, swimming soon became the popular sport. From early morning till late in the evening, and indeed often by moonlight, there seemed always to be someone splashing about in the pools, which were much warmer than the canal. No one will ever forget the Somme, whose shell-scarred valleys have seen some of the fiercest and most stubborn fighting of the war. And of all the troops who contested the Hun advance along that historic river, it is indisputable that for Australians, more so than for any other troops, the Somme holds great associations. Australian battalions fought there early in 1916 and all through the hot summer months, achieving success after success, and now we had come to carry on, and after three months spent in looking up the long line of the canal, with its towpath and avenue of tall trees, we felt a desire to see more of it, to repay

Fritz in kind, driving him back and away from the Somme valley ; a wish we were to fulfil, later, to our great satisfaction.

Nowhere, not even in England, can greater profusion of flower colours be found than on the Somme. Yellow mustard, blue cornflowers, scarlet poppies, and other bright blooms flourish in fallow and cultivated land as if thickly sown there, making pictures that would grace the finest collection of landscape scenes. The artist of our sister battalion, the 42nd, took full advantage of the opportunity afforded him, and those who in the future may be privileged to obtain a view of his work may get some idea—if they have not been there—of the appearance of the Somme Valley in summer.

Our "C" echelon was established at Lamotte Brebiere, three miles down the river from Blangy-Tronville. Even in this peaceful spot, Fritz could not let us have rest for long, and shelled in our vicinity with "india-rubbers." Much of this, however, was directed at the "Queen Mary," one of our largest guns, which fired occasional shots from its railway emplacement near Glisy into targets 36 kilometres (22 miles) away. In accordance with long-established custom the battalion supplied working-parties daily. These were engaged in burying cables. The remainder carried on with specialist training. Almost nightly heavily laden enemy bombing 'planes passed overhead on their way to back areas, but did not disturb us, though "C" echelon occasionally "had the wind up."

The continued fine weather made aerial work possible, and the fullest advantage of it was taken by airmen on both sides. A number of enemy 'planes were brought down, and one of our own machines, a "dolphin," crashed near "C" Company's trenches, the pilot having a miraculous escape.

The 37th Battalion, 10th Brigade, handed over to us the sector we previously occupied at Villers Bretonneux, the relief being completed by 2 a.m., 23rd June.

It was a warm, serene afternoon, the sun shining through a haze, when a party of specialists of the battalion we were relieving in Villers Bretonneux brought back scenes of the drought-stricken West to our minds, and bewilderment to the Tommy gunners from an adjacent 60-pounder battery, who heard their remark. One of these specialists, a Lewis gunner, heavily laden, and perspiring profusely, on seeing us watching their approach, came out with " Hey ! mate, how far is it to the next waterhole."

This turn-in was more satisfactory in regard to work done. As familiarity with the sector increased, we were able to get enemy posts, machine guns, and batteries "shot up," and our artillery, trench-mortars, and machine guns had plenty to do.

"Diggers" will remember the hedge above the railway station where our trench-mortars were concealed. One never knew when enemy retaliation might fall there, so the pace livened up when passing. The first time the front line tranquility was seriously disturbed occurred during this trip in, a trial of the new message rockets being the cause. "C" Company got the blame for drawing the "crabs." These rockets have a hollow rod in which the message is placed, and on the point a siren that, during flight, makes a noise not unlike that caused by a small shell. As it leaves the ground it emits a dense volume of white smoke. Fritz showed his disapproval of the fireworks display in a most vicious manner, putting, in little more than an hour, over seven hundred 5.9's into our front and support lines.

Two raids were carried out by the French on our right, our artillery, trench-mortars, and machine guns, lending some weight with a protective barrage. The French then holding the sector on our right were the 3rd Zouaves, a body consisting largely of Algerians.

Relief came on the 27th, the battalion being lucky in getting clear of the village without suffering casualties, for all the roads were now subjected nightly to heavy shelling.

We slept for the night in old positions at Blangy-Tronville and next day proceeded to Frechencourt, *via* Bussy-les-Daours and Querrieu.

Shelters at Frechencourt were poor, but the "Diggers" are good foragers, and it was not long before dugouts were greatly improved with "salvaged" material.

During our two periods spent at Villers Bretonneux we collected as much salvage as could be transported. Casualties were heavy, most of them being caused by the gas strafe. Now that winter was well over, the health of the battalion was much better than when we were north of the Somme, where many were evacuated sick.

The end of June found us rapidly becoming fit for our turn to push, which, according to "furphies," would come any day, and continue to some indefinite date in the far future, by which "endurance would be taxed to the utmost."

It is certain that no one was sorry to get a chance to win back lost territory. We were heartily tired of "stationary" warfare. As one remarked: "We've come to *fight* Fritz, not to stand about in the trenches waiting to be killed by his artillery, or freeze to death."

When the month closed the whole battalion was eagerly discussing the rumour that we were to "hop the bags" with the Americans.

PHASE VIII.

CHAPTER I.

In "Possies" above Frechencourt.—Preparations for Offensive.—The Americans.—The Glorious 4th July.—Hamel Victory.—Frechencourt Again.—"Bangalow Terrace."—Corbie, Preparations for 8th August.

It was towards the end of June that the battalion finally shook off the dust of Villers Bretonneux, after five comparatively quiet days in the line—

"Where the larks trilled in the sunshine,
Hovering o'er the lines;
Caring naught for bombs or minnies,
Scorning five-point-nines,"

and marched back to the ridge above Frechencourt. "Possies" were quickly fixed up along the banks on the chalk-scarred slope, and brief training for a big stunt commenced. It is interesting to recall that many were looking forward even as early in the summer as this to going back very shortly for the "Corps rest," and perhaps it was just as well for our peace of mind that we could not foresee what the next three months were to bring forth.

From our position we commanded a fine prospect of the Somme Valley, the villages of Frechencourt and Behencourt appearing as clusters of red and white amid the tall trees, which follow the winding of the canal, and beyond, a vista of green slopes with splashes of scarlet poppies shading into purple with the cornflowers—a peaceful pastoral scene, where only the zig-zagging chalky trenches struck a jarring note: those miles of reserve trenches, which, thank Heaven, we never had to use.

This July is memorable for the continuity of fine, warm weather which favoured the whole series of operations that commenced with the advance at Hamel on 4th July, Before the day came, a body of American troops of the 131st Regiment joined us. Our battalion at this time was only three companies strong, "A" Company being practically non-existent after the gassing at Villers Bretonneux, so a composite company was formed, and known as "X" Company, one platoon of "Yanks" being included in this, and one platoon in each of the other companies. The Americans were given a very hearty welcome, and quickly fraternised with the Aussies. The morning parade on the 2nd was, therefore, of more than usual interest, and we had an opportunity of witnessing how the latest army in France carried out an advance in open order.

After conferences and reconnaissances with regard to the impending operations, the whole battalion marched to La Neuville in the evening, and spent the night in trenches there. The following day word came through that the American troops were not to participate in the stunt, but were to return to Allonville. This was a matter for great regret, the Yanks being very disappointed, as they were extraordinarily keen on having a go at the Hun, and were really proud of being allowed to fight alongside Australians. A few, however, co-operated with the 42nd and acquitted themselves well. The approach march, starting at 8.30 p.m., skirted Corbie, two companies following the towpath of the Somme Canal and crossing opposite Hamelet by means of a narrow bridge supported on barrels, the other two companies taking the main road north of the Somme and crossing the canal near Vaire-sous-Corbie chateau. A communication trench at the eastern end of Hamelet led to the reserve line, where the men took up their position without any trouble or casualties, although the usual desultory fire was being carried out by the artillery.

Being in reserve this time we had a splendid view of the initial operations; especially "B" Company, which was in the most advanced position. Before our artillery commenced a harassing fire, to drown the noise of approaching tanks, there was a marked stillness over everything, like the calm before a storm. From information culled from officers captured later, the enemy seems to have suspected nothing. To prevent the approach of the tanks being heard low-flying aeroplanes were also used, and proved very successful. The harassing fire commenced eight minutes before zero hour.

At 3.10 a.m. our barrage dropped, the first round being a smoke shell. It was a magnificent barrage, very even throughout, only a few shells falling short, but of course it was nothing to the inferno that our massed guns used to let loose at Ypres. The 42nd advanced on the left of Hamel, which was left for the 43rd to "mop up." No great opposition was encountered, the "blue line"—the objective—being taken and consolidation commenced. The 44th battalion "leap-frogged" the 43rd and attained the ridge beyond Hamel. It was a truly wonderful sight watching the tanks creeping over the ground through the grey mists of dawn, and the long line of flashing shell-bursts as the barrage lifted and lengthened, while the colossal din of the whole titanic combat smote upon the ears and set the heart palpitating with awe and tense excitement.

The method of attack was briefly as follows:—After the first four minutes the barrage lifted one hundred yards, and the attack moved forward at the rate of one hundred yards every three minutes until east of the church in Hamel, where there was a halt of ten minutes before the advance continued.

HAMEL — 4th July, 1918.

The first intimation of success reached the 43rd Battalion about an hour and a-quarter after zero.

The news was that Hamel had been cleared of the enemy, and that the attack was progressing favourably. This message was sent by signal rocket, and was confirmed by a returning tank.

Two platoons of the 42nd, who were posted south of Bouzencourt, outside the barrage limit, joined in the attack, when the barrage reached them, going forward with the rest, and by 4.30 seven of our tanks could be seen on the ridge near the final objective. This was the first occasion on which we worked in close co-operation with the tanks. They did invaluable work, keeping close up to our barrage and effectively smothering hostile strong posts. Also they successfully established dumps of ammunition, bombs, rations, and water. It was found too that infantry officers can "speak" to tanks on the field and direct them to whatever spot they wish. It is worthy of note that every tank participating in this stunt was eventually brought back safely, though one or two had to be towed. Aeroplanes, among their other activities, dropped parachutes with boxes of ammunition attached, and even Fritz's airmen over Vaire Wood were generous enough to drop supplies in the same way for our men, thinking they were Germans.

One of our airmen was unfortunate when releasing a parachute, which caught on one of the wings. The intrepid observer crawled out on the wing to release it, but was unable to do so before the machine "crashed."

During the stunt prisoners came in in fair numbers. Owing to the success of the whole attack, the 41st Battalion was not required to take an active part, and so we remained in support, "B" Company moving up at night and digging trenches north of Notamel Wood. "C" Company took up positions south of Hamel and occupied our old front line. On the Saturday evening before we left the battle-ground Fritz sent us over plenty of H.E. and ground shrapnel, making things pretty lively for the platoons dug in on the flat, but Hamel itself came in for the largest share. Here, fortunately, the shells could do very little more damage than had already been done, as our men gave the village a wide berth. During the battle a great part of the place was in flames, but amid the dense volumes of smoke the tricolour flag of victory fluttered in the breeze from a shattered roof-top, where some enterprising soldier had climbed while the Huns were being ferreted out of their dugouts and cellars. Hamel was a complete ruin.

Our appointed task accomplished, we marched back again to La Neuville and the chalk quarry, and then on to the hillside above Frechencourt, where the observation balloon, high above the valley, had overlooked the scene of the great battle, directing the artillery to the best advantage.

In the Hamel stunt the battalion only lost one man killed and eight wounded.

For a few days we resumed training. There was also football and bathing and a good pierrot show, and then, on the 12th July, we were again on the move. A day or two before, however, many will remember well the alarm one evening, when the battalion was suddenly ordered to pack up and to be ready to move within an hour—"action front." Some were down in the villages and many at a concert in Behencourt at the time, and on returning leisurely up the hill to their "possies" received quite a shock at seeing the companies assembled in full fighting order. Even the packs and blankets were handed in to be stored and the cookers made tea for the men. But there was "nothing doing" after all. It was a practice stunt, to see how quickly the battalion could pack up and get on the move in case of necessity. The new "possies" to which we marched from Frechencourt were at "Bangalow Terrace," among the howitzers of the 107th and 126th Batteries. Two companies occupied the old reserve line in front of Hamelet. At Bangalow Terrace there were chalk trenches and strong dugouts all along the escarpments. The battalion was nominally in reserve here, but the days were fairly quiet, comparatively few shells falling near our positions. Every day there was swimming in the Somme, and at night there were working-parties wiring, burying cables, and building or enlarging dugouts. A working-party in summer time, when the ground is dry, and the nights fairly warm, is a very ordinary affair compared with the trail through the mud of Messines, where the rain and sleet used to lash the face continually, and where a slip off the duckboards—if there were any—would send one floundering in a morass knee-deep; those were nights of fearful memory, when shells were only a minor worry. But down there, in front of Corbie that summer, conditions were good and Fritz very lenient.

Perhaps the only difficulty that confronted the trench-digger was a hard seam of chalk, and on this account many a length of cable rested nearer the surface than the regulations provided for, but, "Ca ne fait rien," they served their purpose, and before long Fritz was well on the run from that region. Bangalow Terrace remained our Headquarters till August. Enemy airmen, taking advantage of white billowy clouds, ventured over now and again, keeping well above them, and in this way succeeded in bringing down in flames some of our balloons. One evening four "sausages" were brought down thus in quick succession. From our hillside possie we had a " dress circle " view of the spectacle, and could plainly discern the parachute descents of the balloon occupants. And then on the return of the raiders our Lewis guns would join with the " Archies " in the barrage, which sounded deadly enough to bring anything down, and yet so often failed to prevent the airman's escape. But our anti-aircraft machine gun registered a hit that evening and a loud cheer rang forth as the plane, now flying low to avoid the shells, was seen to " wobble " when directly over our heads and dive forward ; but the pilot still had sufficient control to " carry on " for a while, and, when the machine disappeared from view over the ridge, the betting was ten to one on his having crashed to earth within our lines. On 4th August the battalion crossed the Somme and bivouacked in an orchard behind a massive stone wall some fifteen feet high, probably the remains of some old abbey precincts, on the eastern outskirts of Corbie. This ancient town had been greatly damaged by shell-fire, but the solid towers of the western front of the old Abbaye still stand almost intact, though one side of the church has collapsed entirely, filling the building with a heap of fallen masonry.

To make shelters for ourselves, we had to ransack this part of the town again, and all day long men could be seen with pieces of galvanised iron, doors, shutters, bedsteads, curtains, and all manner of odds and ends, which would make their temporary dwellings more comfortable, and incidentally increase the subsequent bill for damages " apres la guerre." About this time a familiar sight in the streets of Corbie was our " Salvage King," " Bob " Perkins, pushing his hand-barrow along, laden with coal or other useful commodities. This lad, bronzed by summer sun, and whose brawny arms and " nuggetty " figure testified to a strength above the average, proved himself invaluable to the 41st. One had only to wish for something in his hearing, and lo ! a little later he would turn up with any amount of the stuff required, collected as by magic from Heaven knows where. Not only at Corbie, but wherever the battalion went, our salvage expert carried on his useful trade. He was wounded for the second time on 8th August, and so the battalion lost his services. He certainly " did his bit " in more ways than one.

The next two or three days we spent in preparation for the great push. There were conferences for the officers, who passed on information in lecturettes to the men. There was a practice stunt, over a replica of our objective and the country we were going to operate on, made to scale on the ground near the camp. Numerous photos of the enemy positions, taken from aeroplanes were studied, and helped to give a better idea of what would be required of us.

Every night during our stay in Corbie, Fritz kept us aware of his presence by sending over various types of shells. Some " lobbed " fairly near our billets, and the Q.M. store, which is usually considered rather a safe retreat, chanced one night to " stop " a gas shell, which unfortunately incapacitated some of the staff, and caused one fatal casualty. The same night, as the battalion moved out in fighting order, one of the observation balloons, which had been brought up well forward, hung low over the trees some distance to the east of the town, obscured from Fritz's view by the evening mists, and ready to ascend in the early hours of the following morning when the barrage opened.

CHAPTER 2.

The Great Advance.—Stunts of 8th and 11th August, 1918.—Camped in Valley behind Hamel.

At midnight on the 7th-8th August we left Corbie, and in pitch darkness floundered through muddy paths on the low, lagoon-studded ground of the Somme, to the pontoon bridge, thrown across the stream that night near Hamelet.

All routes were crammed with troops making their way up for the surprise attack in the morning, and the thousands of men, horses, and vehicles, on other duties attendant thereon, ebbed and flowed like the sea. Owing to the congestion in the traffic, our progress was necessarily slow, but we passed through Hamelet and Hamel, and reached our assembly tape on Hamel Hill, in rear of the 44th Battalion, an hour before zero. Before continuing, a brief outline of what was happening may be of interest. After the wonderful success of the 4th of July, and owing to the high morale of the Australian troops, the Higher Command saw that if the troops who were holding the line were to make an attack, it had a fair chance of being a complete surprise and consequently a success, as the Boche would never dream that " tired " troops, who had been aggressively holding the line since March without rest, could turn round and attack them. They would at least expect fresh Divisions to take over the line, before there would be any change in the situation. Another point of interest is, that this " Big Break-through " was the first occasion on which the whole Australian Corps had been employed together, and we felt confident of the result. The left flank of the Corps rested on the Somme and the right on the Villers Bretonneux-Rosieres Railway, where we joined on to the Canadians. North of the Somme, our flank was protected by the 174th British Brigade, who were to advance in conformity with our movements. The 3rd Division held the post of honour on the north of the Corps, and had to take, in conjunction with the 2nd Division on its right, the objective, the " green " line, which ran just west of Cerisy-Gailly, and was a penetration of some four thousand yards. The 4th and 5th Divisions were then to " leap-frog " through them, and fight their way to the old French trench-system, which lay another five thousand yards to the east. Along the Somme the 42nd had a narrow frontage, and consequently had to go the whole distance. South of them the 44th Battalion had to take up to the vicinity of Gailly, known as the " red " line, and the 41st were to go through them and capture the " green " line. Operating on our south was our 9th Brigade. Practically in the centre of the battalion on its assembly tape, Battalion Headquarters were established, in the old trench-system east of Hamel. About 4.5 a.m., a quarter of an hour before zero, the enemy artillery became very active on this ridge, due no doubt to the noise made by approaching tanks, which were distinguishable above the droning of the engines of low-flying aeroplanes, and an anxious time was experienced until our barrage dropped, up to time. The artillery preparation was splendid; the counter-battery work especially was so thorough, that one cannot say the enemy artillery retaliation was severe. A matter of minutes after the show started, the atmosphere was thick with smoke, mist, and H.E., which reduced the visibility to some ten or fifteen yards. This state of affairs was just as we wished, as it gave us an opportunity to close on enemy machine guns practically unseen. The greatest trouble experienced was keeping direction, and many can bless the Hamel-Cerisy road running on our left flank, which gave them a clue to their whereabouts, for those who got lost wandered on to its paved surface, and soon found their bearings again. As regards the " mopping up," no serious difficulties were experienced, for as soon as sounds of resistance reached the ears of sections pushing forward in this murky pandemonium, they closed in on the fighting—and that meant the end of the garrison. In the mist, Captain French and C.S.M. Burnett came suddenly on an enemy battery in action, and gallantly mopped up the outfit, taking some twenty prisoners. For this and other useful work they received a bar to the M.C. and a Military Medal respectively. The runners coming back with messages had the utmost difficulty in finding Battalion Headquarters, and all information as to progress was practically obtained by questioning prisoners and their escorts, or from our wounded.

Prisoners came back in an unending stream, and when, on questioning some, it was found that they were captured in the vicinity of where we were establishing the " green " line, the Battalion Headquarters were moved forward to Kate Wood. On the left, " D " and " B " Companies reached their objectives to time, and the two right companies, " A " and " C," captured their line later on, and immediately sent a party forward under Lieutenant J. Lawson with the tanks to mop up Forbes and Hamilton Woods, which were strongly held by the enemy. This enterprise was highly successful, and yielded about two hundred prisoners and a few field guns. By this time our casualties had not been very heavy, but the mist being dispelled by the morning sun, we began to get shelled from batteries north of the river firing with open sights. This unfortunate state of affairs was the result of the British troops failing to get their objectives. Machine guns from Cerisy itself also were troublesome, and our casualties began to mount up.

Our Pioneer Battalions did good work, repairing roads, in some cases only a few hundred yards behind the advance. This enabled motor and heavy traffic to move forward to programme. At 9 a.m. the 4th Division moved through, and claimed the attention of the aforesaid batteries. One of the finest sights of the War was the "leap-frogging" divisions moving forward to the attack. This was our first glimpse of open warfare.

Looking back towards Hamel, as far as eye could reach, in lines of sections in single file, the battalions moved forward with sections of machine gunners and trench-mortars with their weapons; while dotted here and there were lumbering tanks. Behind these waves of men were long streams—which were lost in the horizon—of artillery teams with guns, engineers with all their paraphernalia, balloons being towed by lorries, pack mules, wagons, horsemen, and laden lorries; a vast congregation, all with their special duties to perform, to ensure the success of the venture.

Around Cerisy we watched with interest our ranks dealing with strong points, nosing them out like terriers do rats, and triumphantly playing with them, as their six-pounders got to work and silenced these nests for all time. As the leading avalanche moved through us, our men in their half-finished trenches stood up and cheered them on. Some facts regarding this great advance which may be of interest, are, that the battalion put over some four hundred and eighty actual fighting men, and with this number penetrated some one thousand five hundred yards, and took an objective with a frontage of a mile, which is no mean feat. Also, besides inflicting casualties on the enemy estimated at six to one, we captured nine field guns, twenty machine guns, and five trench-mortars. Our casualties were approximately one hundred, and amongst the noble company who lie for ever by the Somme, we left a favourite officer, "Bluey" Roberts.

During the day we consolidated our position, and the company of the 43rd Battalion loaned to us as support company in the valley west of Kate Wood gave us great assistance in burying our dead and tidying things up generally. Next day passed fairly quietly. In the morning an enterprising 'plane came over and destroyed one of our observation balloons. We were so accustomed to seeing aeronauts descending in parachutes, like thistle-down in the wind, that it is to be feared that these unfortunates never got their true measure of sympathy from the "Digger," who looked on these matters as interesting interludes in a day's work. On this occasion, the 'plane which did the damage was shot down by machine-gun fire, the "Archies," of course, giving a hand, and no doubt destroying his morale. In the afternoon the fight north of the Somme was viewed by us with more than passing interest, as our friends of the 4th July, the 131st U.S. Regiment, were engaged. We learnt afterwards that the stunt was fairly successful, but, as we had expected, their objective was obtained at terrible cost. During this fight our men, only too keen to assist their "Yank" friends, wheeled round the captured guns in the Cerisy Valley, and, under an artillery officer, put up a strafe on the enemy's back areas. On the following day we received instructions to go forward and relieve the 13th Battalion, 4th Division, in the front line. Immediately a reconnaissance was made, and at dusk the battalion moved out and completed the relief by midnight. The enemy artillery, on this march in darkness, kept one reminded that there was still a war on, and many must have heaved a sigh of relief when the passage through Morcourt, where hostile 'planes dropped bomb after bomb, was safely negotiated.

Battalion Headquarters were located in one of these gullies peculiar to the Somme, some eight hundred yards in rear of the line. It was not exactly a healthy spot, as German gunners, with time on their hands, select these spots for shoots "off the map," and one unaware of the locality of Battalion Headquarters, only had to go towards the heaviest-strafed area in the valley, and there he would find it.

Here is a little story related in connection with the 8th August stunt. An Auusie was escorting back a Boche prisoner, who, so far from carrying an extra pair of boots with him, as many did, had not even a pair to walk in. The couple were met by a "Woodbine," who passed some jocular remark abour Fritz's deficiency, upon which the Aussie "chipped" in with, "It's all right mate, he wore his boots out chasing you chaps up." On the 11th August we were established in the old French system of trenches east of Morcourt, with the left flank refused west of Mericourt. The 43rd Battalion held the line on the left, and the 42nd on the right. In the course of the morning, word came through that we had to capture, that evening, the portion of the trench-system from the road running past St. Germain's Wood to the bank of the Somme, which was held by the Boche, and effect a junction with the 4th Division north of the Somme. This meant that we had to break through the enemy lines, cutting off his troops in that formidable Cateaux Wood and Mericourt-sur-Somme, and hold these trenches against attacks from front and rear until the situation was cleared behind us.

The operation, on first thought, appeared suicidal; but on further consideration appeared to have a fair chance of success, owing to its very boldness and the great element of surprise. Although time was limited, full arrangements were made, which if they had been carried out, would have saved us many valuable lives. Broadly the arrangements were, that the artillery and machine guns were to put a standing barrage on both sides of the trenches parallel to our advance, and we would follow a "creeping" barrage moving in front of us at the rate of one hundred yards in four minutes. At the same time Mericourt would be bombarded by the trench-mortars, and the light mortars would accompany the attackers. We were offered tanks, but refused them, for many reasons. It was ticklish business getting the three companies "A," "B," and "D," who were assaulting, into the assembly positions without the enemy's knowledge, but in the course of the afternoon the move was carried out successfully, and the reserve company, "C," held the front.

While the three companies awaited zero hour, a general fear was that enemy 'planes would come over and locate this gathering, and all felt relieved when a strong scout patrol, with the familar concentric markings, flew overhead.

The trench to be captured was divided into three parts: the portion adjacent to the Somme was "A" Company's share in the enterprise, and "D" Company's sector came next, with "B" Company's on the right. At 8.30 p.m. the "Show" started and the attackers moved out in skirmishing order. The support given by the artillery was disappointing, being so feeble that it could not be called a barrage. Being once committed to the venture, no one had a thought of turning back, but pressed forward in short rushes, calling into play all experiences and lessons learnt in former fights. In spite of terrific machine-gun fire from all flanks and in front, they won through with bomb and bayonet, and the help of the trench-mortars. As we had expected, darkness came to our aid and enabled our men to close with the enemy. Time and time again, deeds of valour were performed, amongst which Lieutenant Joe Woodford's noble self-sacrifice stands out conspicuously. This brave officer, giving his life for his platoon, rushed a machine gun, that was holding them up, from the front, thus allowing his platoon to come in from the flanks.

The fight raged for forty-five minutes, and then the green success rockets soared up from the region of the Somme. The holding of these captured trenches during the night is worthy of note. Each company had three platoons facing the east, and one facing the west, to guard against counter-attacks likely to be made by the enemy.

Throughout the night these garrisons also kept capturing Huns, and in Cateaux Wood, a party of two officers and seventy of other ranks surrendered to a post belonging to "A" Company.

This fight, which ranks as the best single-handed endeavour the battalion ever engaged in, cost us seventy-five men and five officers, but we took in prisoners alone over two hundred men, besides wounding and killing over one hundred of the enemy. The trench-mortars under Lieutenant "Dave" Brown did splendid work, and this sterling officer, who died from wounds received in this fight, had the Military Cross conferred upon him. Amongst those who worthily merited—and in some cases received—recognition, were—"Bluey" Walker, "D.C.M."; Captain P. F. Calow, "M.C."; Lieutenant J. Grant Smith, "M.C."; Lieutenant J. J. Hanley; and Lieutenant E. D. Price, "M.C."

The result of our successful enterprise was, that on the following day the 43rd Battalion, using prisoners as informers, were able to mop up the encircled country and effect the capture of the enemy troops without casualty. In the afternoon of the 12th, we received instructions that we had to attack, with the 42nd on our right and the Somme on our left flank, and capture the railheads with its dumps and the high ground west of Chuignolles. Owing to the heavy fighting of the previous night, we decided for this purpose to employ the company of the 43rd under Captain Oswald, M.C., which was attached to us. This company, after suffering severely from shell-fire, effected a junction with the 42nd, who had had heavy fighting in the vicinity of St. Germain's Wood. That night we were relieved by battalions of the 17th Division, and moved back to the line we had occupied on the 8th, south of Cerisy-Gailly. On the march back we were troubled by enemy aircraft bombing the roads, but the battalion's luck in this respect stood us in good stead. The following day the battalion moved again to a valley before Hamel, where "possies" were dug in the escarpments. This valley debouched on the Somme, and all, in their unwashed condition, were glad to get down there for a swim in the lagoons. Some indulged in a pastime, very popular until stopped, known as fishing, using "Fritz" stick-handle bombs, which one could find lying about all over the hillside where the "hop-over" had started. While we were spelling here, the whole of the echelon, that had been following up in the rear from the vicinity of Bussy to Hamelet, now joined the main body of the battalion, and our depleted ranks were also swelled by a large draft of reinforcements. A conference of Company Commanders and Headquarters Staffs took place one day at Brigade Headquarters on the hill on the opposite side of the valley, to discuss a proposed operation in the Harbonnieres area, but this was afterwards cancelled. Hostile aircraft were active at night, but no bombs fell near to our bivouacs. Many will remember sitting, sometimes for hours, without a light, when the throb of the engines could be heard in the stillness of the night. The battalion was now reorganised, and after a well-deserved rest a limited amount of training was carried on.

The 11th Brigade Pierrots entertained us one evening, and a good show was provided by Lieutenants Boorman and Lewis, of the 42nd Battalion. The latter, to our extreme regret, was killed in the Quarry Farm stunt of 1st September. On Sunday, the 18th, the first church parade for many a long day was held, and then came reconnaissances across the canal—a sure sign of a speedy move.

CHAPTER 3.

In the Valley North of Sailly-Laurette.—Forward to Gressaire Wood, near Etinehem.—Dugouts.—The Advance Through Bray to Susanne.—Maricourt Valley.—Our Two Advances in One Day.—Vaux Wood.—Fargny Mill: Gordon Wins the "V.C." —How We Captured the Motor-car.—Dug-in in Copse Valley.—On Through Ruined Curlu to Hem.

On the 19th August we crossed once more to the north of the Somme, camping in what we afterwards called "Balloon Valley," a narrow re-entrant winding in from the canal near Sailly-Laurette. By this time we were getting used to digging possies and were quite adept at it, the only trouble being the scarcity sometimes of suitable roofing.

In this connection it is worthy of note that many an excellent dugout, carefully made by some previous builder, has been unroofed and pulled to pieces to help construct a new one only a few hundred yards away. Artillery units were also camped in this valley, and a balloon; and looking down from the hillside the scene was full of life and bustle—horses, mules, limbers, and all the paraphernalia of war crowded together in the narrow basin.

It is of interest to record that this gully was formerly the scene of many an outpost skirmish in March of the same year. There along the ridge was the old front-line trench, and near the road, which crossed the valley further up from our bivouac, a few white crosses marked the last resting-places of a few of our comrades.

The march forward on the 22nd was begun in the early hours before the mist had lifted. Just before the start the stillness of the morning was suddenly broken by the thunderous reverberations of the big guns further up the Somme Valley, as the barrage commenced for the day's advance. This was an almost daily occurrence, for

Marshal Foch, now in supreme command of the Allied Forces in France, saw to it that Fritz was given no rest. In fact, the enemy never knew where the blow might fall next. The advance once begun had to be continued until the scourge was driven clean out of the land.

Through the red dust of battered Sailly-Laurette, along the river road, the column went forward through country which but a few days ago had been in German hands, to which the wayside dumps of whizz-bang shells in their wicker cases and frequent German signboards bore ample testimony.

The artillery was still blazing away as we passed near some 9.2 batteries, and further on we halted for a while amid massed active howitzers. The valley we were following had narrowed considerably, and soon we found ourselves in a wood, where the stench of modern war assailed the nostrils in the form of gas, which hung about the newer shell-holes in the dewy atmosphere, causing general involuntary sneezing.

Wounded artillerymen were being brought back down the track, some on stretchers, and we heard a few remarks about batteries being blown up by Fritz's retaliating fire. In Gressaire Wood, Battalion Headquarters was established, the companies being posted on the ridges slightly in advance. Our battalion was in reserve to the 11th Brigade, and, in case we should be required, tactical schemes were discussed at a conference of Company Commanders on the following day. From the moment of our arrival and throughout the day H.E. shells were falling along the track, through the wood, and in front of the company-positions. Nine casualties resulted, one shell unfortunately striking a dugout and killing three men of "D" Company. The town of Etinehem lay down in the valley over beyond our right post. Here, as at many other stages in our advance, we found large German dugouts, some of them forming a sort of underground system, and all having steep well-revetted shafts. It was fairly obvious that Fritz intended to settle down in these "possies" for the winter, if possible, and judging by the number of our 'planes that used to cross over to bomb his lines he badly needed refuges of this kind. Dugouts were many and varied in some sectors; in others practically non-existent. Fritz is a great believer in dugouts, especially the shell-and-bomb-proof, thirty-feet-deep kind. That was the sort Headquarters used to look for during an advance but would never inhabit until one or two engineers had first been down below and returned safe and intact up the steps and reported "all well." For we were all very wise soon after the big advance commenced, and left severely alone any attractive souvenir which looked at all suspicious of concealing some diabolical Hun-trap, while newly-captured dugouts were regarded with suspicion until some authority had taken the risk of inspecting them. But who will ever forget our own dugouts—so called; for instance, at Armentieres? What crude makeshifts they were, those muddy shelters, where rats and "chats" made things so lively for the "Diggers" within! Two men would occupy these funk-holes, the longer of the two stretching his legs out through the low entrance, often tripping up men as they passed along the trench outside. The rain penetrated into these hovels and covered blankets and everything else with wet mud. The funk-holes in the line at Villers Bretonneux, gouged out of the trench-wall, were inferior even to those; but it was summer then, and the ground was dry. Some men "have been honoured" with the title of "dugout king." These men were the envy of the platoons in the front trenches, and were generally supposed to quaff S.R.D. all day long, being held responsible for the general shortage of this beverage. They often objected to the overcrowding of their domain during an extra big strafe or when Fritz 'planes came over laying eggs. But all this is by the way. On the 24th we moved again. There was no rest during that last big push, and we had a long way yet to go to the Hindenburg line. The next "possies" was in the neighbourhood of Bray, not far from the railway. The following morning's attack was successful, the 42nd and 43rd digging-in on the high ridge, whence one could look across to Maricourt and Suzanne. Light horsemen worked in conjunction with the infantry, doing fine scouting work and helping to keep up communications. Shells were falling freely along the ridge where they were operating. Our battalion soon found this out when a forward move was made. The shelling continued throughout the day. The following is a brief summary of the operations:—On the 25th, before mid-day, the battalion moved forward on to the ridge, then occupied by the 42nd and 43rd. On reaching the crest of the hill they were met with a heavy barrage from machine guns and field guns firing from short range, and quickly took cover. Our battalion remained in close touch with the 42nd and with the 10th Brigade on the right, and with English troops on the left. Despite the heavy shelling all day our casualties were not numerous. The light horse tried to advance but were held up by hostile fire. As it was considered unwise to advance during daylight without artillery support, at 5 p.m. we returned to the "possies" of the previous night. During the night the 43rd and 44th advanced their line slightly, and on the following day the battalion again moved forward to the reserve position it had previously occupied. About mid-day, the 10th and 11th Brigades attacked, and pushed the line forward to the edge of Vaux Wood, but machine guns hidden in the huts overlooking Maricourt Valley held up the 43rd Battalion. And now came our turn. We had to make two separate advances across some rather difficult country. After crossing the Maricourt Valley there was the ridge where the hut encampment was situated, with the dark mass of Vaux Wood beyond. From this further ridge the ground fell steeply away down towards Fargny and Curlu, which lie almost at the bottom of a deep gorge. The first order received was that we should relieve the 43rd, but during the afternoon these instructions were altered, and accordingly the battalion moved forward that night through the 43rd, forming a line well in advance of them, and in touch with the 44th. By 2.50 a.m. the success-signal was sent up in the form of green Verey lights. During this night advance orders came through that the battalion would have to be ready at 4.55 to take part in a general attack in conjucntion with the 58th British Division. This included the taking of Maricourt by the British on our left. The 10th Brigade had already mopped up Suzanne.

Between Maricourt and Fargny there was a trench-system, and it was part of our job to oust the Hun from their stronghold, of which Fargny Mill was, perhaps, the chief point. At any rate, for us the name will be for ever memorable for the bravery and initiative displayed by Private Gordon ("C" Company), better known as "Bernie" Gordon, who, we are proud to relate, was awarded the V.C.

There was a particularly offensive machine-gunner, who was also a persistently accurate marksman. Gordon went out and shot the offender, and captured the gun and crew of nine, together with an officer, single-handed. All through the stunt this same man was conspicuous for the work he did, and it was mainly owing to his initiative that the thick nests of machine guns in front of our objective were effectively stamped out. These machine guns were so lively that it was almost impossible to move about in the vicinity of the objective. But in the afternoon their stings were drawn, Gordon repeatedly going into Fargny Wood to souvenir some of these objectionable creatures. In all, he captured during the stunt sixty prisoners, two officers, and six machine guns. Everyone knows that V.C.'s have been won over and over again in operations such as these, and often not even a Military Medal has fallen to the lot of those who have fully merited the higher distinction. Most of the 41st Battalion know "Bluey" Walker, D.C.M., and no one could deny that he also fully earned a V.C., particularly for the work he did on the 11th and 12th of August in the Mericourt stunt, when he wiped out enemy machine-gun posts single-handed, rushing forward with his Lewis gun held at the hip, and firing as he ran.

In this battle, our own machine guns were more than unally active, and the trench-mortars, working in conjunction, gave great assistance in exterminating these nests of Boches. They concentrated upon and silenced enemy gunners on the Chapeau de Gendarme.

Sniping was another source of trouble to the platoons in the front positions, but fortunately we had the superiority here. In spite of the heavy fighting, the battalion only sustained about forty casualties. It was during this stunt that we scored our motor-lorry or ambulance, it being used for Red Cross work by the Germans. The actual honour and glory for this most useful capture fell to the lot of No. 6 Platoon, led by Lieutenant C. H. Butler, to whom the driver surrendered after being held up in the good old highwayman fashion. This car, which the 11th Field Ambulance kept in running order for a while, proved a most valuable asset to the battalion, when we finally left the line and went back for our rest. At Walrus it made an excellent green-grocery vehicle, and the sergeant cook was able to travel far and wide over the country on his quest for supplementary rations. Later still, at St. Maxent, despite a temporary disappearance about Christmas time and numerous breakdowns, with a new cover and bright coat of green, the old car did many a trip between the officers' mess and Abbeville. Beside the car, we captured one hundred prisoners and twenty machine guns.

The whole operation ranks with the Mericourt stunt as one of the finest and most difficult carried out by the battalion. Barely an hour was given to the company commanders to make arrangements, and there was no reconnaissance of the ground beforehand. The men also were tired, having made an advance of nearly one thousand yards. And when one adds to this the fact that the advance was really a successive movement diagonal to the barrage line, and that the British failed to take the exploitation line as anticipated, which would have relieved our right flank, the brilliant success of this quickly-planned engagement reflects the highest credit on officers and men alike.

After the relief we marched right back to bivouacs near the old B.H.Q., which had been temporarily moved forward just before the last advance. By this time the big guns were well forward, and the close proximity of a battery of 6-inch howitzers made sleep rather spasmodic for some of us, but not even a full barrage would wake an Aussie after many weary days of following up the Hun retreat, finishing off with a stiff " box-on."

When the guns moved forward, it was high time for us to be going, for this valley had already become a semi-back area," and the balloons were almost level with us; and even the canteen had caught us up, much to our delight.

So while the 9th Brigade was carrying on the good work of Boche-chasing, we pushed on behind and established ourselves in the Suzanne-Mericourt Valley in a steep bank full of caves and funk-holes, so that a few of us had no evacuating to do. Copse Valley was our actual position, and Brigade Headquarters were also situated there.

Soon after most of us had sorted ourselves out into our new "possies," the Divisional Commander came round, and an amusing little incident occurred. This personage did not indulge in all the outward insignia usually associated with a "brass hat"; in fact, he wore nothing to mark his rank beyond the tabs on his service tunic and shoulder-straps, which were only discernible at close quarters. He happened thus to stroll up to one "Digger" saying, "Having a good spell"? The "Digger," unaware of the identity of his interlocutor, replied, "Spell be damned!—digging-in six times in three ———— days!"

At the end of August, Major E. J. Dibden, of the 42nd, took over the command of the battalion, as Lieutenant-Colonel Heron went away on English leave. Major A. T. Ferguson was now appointed temporarily to the command of the 43rd Battalion.

We only rested in Copse Valley two days. Breakfast at one o'clock in the morning in pouring rain has not quite the same attraction as a petit dejeuner of hot chocolate in bed in a Paris hotel; indeed, it loses any charm it might possess, when you discover afterwards that you are having a "Buckshee" meal, as it were, the movement order having been cancelled "a la derniere heure."

This is what happened on the penultimate day of the month of August, 1918. The next day saw us well *en route* towards the front again. The descent from the Vaux Wood ridge was rough and steep, and everywhere were signs of the recent conflict. The bodies of German and British troops were strewn all over the plateau between Copse Valley and Maricourt Valley, where the Huns had a temporary trench and many machine-gun posts. In their advance on Maricourt, the Tommies must have suffered heavy casualties, especially across this open ridge. The battalion marched through Curlu.

It was now that we began to realise the extent of our advance, for here we were penetrating into the belt of country which had been devastated in the early days of the war, where towns and villages had been absolutely wiped out of existence, with scarcely a trace left to mark their original site. Curlu was the first village we struck of this kind. Hamel and Sailly-Laurette had been what one would call complete ruins of a sort, but they were almost habitable places compared with those we had now reached—villages which had been practically in the front line for two years. There was nothing to mark the site of Curlu save a small fragment of church and here and there some traces of cellars which had been used as dugouts. All loose débris had been cleared away, the red dust of the main road explaining the disappearance of bricks, while all farm machinery and ironwork had been carefully heaped by Fritz into one huge dump. Yet in this shell-swept area one solitary farmhouse still defied the ravages of war. There it stood, a battered hulk, beyond the eastern end of lost Curlu; we had already passed Fargny Mill—what remained of it—the scene of that heroic struggle two days earlier; and from Curlu we followed the road to Hem. A few long-distance shells were falling ahead of us in the valley, of the armour-piercing variety, the target being a bridge over the canal, which was crowded with guns and transport, all moving forward. Hem was in a similar condition to Curlu; the gateposts of some large houses were still standing, and a fragment of a chateau. We finally came to a halt at Monacu, near an old sugar-mill, where there were trenches and a few dugouts, belonging to the pre-1916 push period, trenches and shell-holes being overgrown with grass and weeds, for—

> " Though raging guns assail the landscape,
> Spreading ruin wide,
> Nature still asserts her empire
> O'er the countryside."

CHAPTER 4.

The Battle of the 1st September, 1918.

The fight of the 1st September will long be remembered as an historical one for the Australian Corps. Our Brigade fought throughout this day on the left flank of the 2nd Division. Our opponents, the Prussian Guards, who, we understood from prisoners, had volunteered to stop the Australians, put up a bitter fight, but were defeated before the sun had set. Names such as Mont. St. Quentin, Haut Allaines, Bouchavesnes, and Moislains, whenever mentioned, will bring back memories of this day. Our approach-march from Monacu was made under a starry heaven. Except for the thought of what lay before us, the four-mile march along a good road would have been pleasant. The route was on the main road to Clery-sur-Somme, to the left up the hill, and along the plateau until the Bapaume-Peronne road was reached; then south, parallel with the road where our assembly place was. To reach the assembly tape, we had to run the usual gauntlet of harassing fire along the roads, but were fortunate in respect to casualties, which were exceedingly light. Towards morning the weather changed, and in drizzling rain we had a long wait for zero hour. It was practically light when the barrage opened, consequently we lost the cover of darkness to close with machine-gun posts, and mighty little cover of any other description could we find. Following the barrage, we crossed the road, and had sharp fighting in the maze of trenches on the forward slope of the hill. The valley was crossed under a hail of machine-gun bullets. Fighting up the reverse slope of the next ridge, touch with the 43rd on the right was lost, and the battalion was drawn to the south, feeling for support on that flank. Captain French immediately pushed up " C " Company and filled the dangerous breach between the 42nd and " D " Company. Heavy fighting took place in the trenches on this ridge, a good deal of it hand-to-hand. At last we won through, and found ourselves in Kassa and Yassa trenches. It was intended, on reaching the objective, that " C " and " A " Companies should leap-frog through " D " and " B " and exploit our success. This was attempted, but on the south it was hopeless. The flank was in the air, and a deadly hail from enemy machine guns situated in the Canal du Nord, Haut Allaines, and Scutari trench forced the company concerned to take cover again in Kassa trench. At this juncture Captain Uren, Lieutenant Mitchell, and Lieutenant Rigg, all fine officers, lost their lives. On the north, " C " Company pushed on about another five hundred yards. Gaining this high ground and finding it madness either to remain or go on, they decided to return to Yassa trench. Thus, surrounded on three sides by the enemy, with the greatest difficulty they reached the trench, carrying their wounded with them. Captain French was now a stretcher case. It is stated that he was wounded by a German who had surrendered. It is also stated that the prisoner and the party to which he belonged will never be able to boast of the deed. And so we lost Captain French, who returned to Australia when he was convalescent. As a Company Commander he was without equal, and as a man and officer universally liked. Consequently his departure from amongst us was keenly felt.

The next consideration was to reorganise. In spite of what was perhaps the heaviest machine-gun fire we have experienced, this was accomplished, and " C " Company went into support in banks in rear of the hill, while " D," " A," and " B " held the front line. From the front line on the forward slope above Haut Allaines a splendid view was obtained, and the enemy in great numbers could be seen moving about in all the copses in front and on the right flank up to Mont St. Quentin, which was not mopped up till the afternoon. All day the slightest movement brought terrific machine-gun fire on that bare hillside. Our men did some good sniping, and, on word being sent back to our artillery, an enemy " whizz-bang," firing through open sights from the railway near Haut Allaines, was subsequently seen to harness up and gallop back to shelter behind Moislains. On the right it was impossible to evacuate our wounded during daylight, and so they lay in the trenches, ministered to by their mates, until nightfall. Stretcher-bearers tried gallantly to get these men away, but immediately they showed themselves they were fired on, and if they persisted on their errands of mercy, they became themselves casualties. All nobly played the game, but the following men and N.C.O.'s were especially noticeable :—Gordon, Webb, Hagger, Mazzer, Woolcock, Follington, Mesh, Lowth, Goodwin, and Harris. Before midnight the Somersets relieved us, with the exception of No. 6 Platoon under Lieutenant C. H. Butler. This platoon, attached to the 43rd Battalion, participated in the attack on Scutari Trench, and we learnt from them that the platoon of only fourteen men did Homeric deeds without suffering any casualties.

One cannot leave the account of this battle without a few concluding remarks. Our artillery barrage was very feeble, owing to most of our guns supporting the "Tommies" on our left and the attack being commenced too late in the morning ; consequently our losses were heavy, being some one hundred and twenty men and five officers, three of whom were killed.

Our frontage was a thousand yards, while a whole British Brigade on our left flank had only twelve hundred yards.

The battalion put about four hundred actual fighting men over the top, and when one considers the number of prisoners taken, approximately two hundred and fifty, besides the number we killed, one must admit we had a strenuous day. Amongst the war trophies captured figured five field guns, two trench-mortars, and forty-five machine-guns. As regards the field guns, the Lewis gunners of " D " Company, appearing on the scene as some of the teams were withdrawing them, mopped-up the outfit.

On relief the battalion moved back to the valley north of Clery.

Enemy aircraft was very active bombing, and our outgoing troops suffered casualties, amongst whom " B " Company's Sergeant-Major, J. Lowth, was killed. Lowth was a man known among all ranks as a fine athlete and sterling N.C.O., both in and out of the line.

In the valley hot tea and food was served, and then companies independently made their way back to Cheesewood, near Hem.

To tired troops the march seemed interminable in the dark, and many will remember the long silent trudge. The dawn of the next day had broken before all the battalion were rolled in their blankets to slumber.

CHAPTER 5.

The Spell at Cheesewood, near Hem.—The Hun's Rapid Retreat.—Forward to Mont St. Quentin and Bussu.—Our Advance Through Tincourt to Roisel.—The Camp at Doingt and Peronne.

The 2nd of September saw the battalion (what was left of it) resting in " possies " near Cheesewood, not far from the now extinct village of Hem. Everyone was tired to the verge of exhaustion, and by mid-day, when the " Diggers " started to move about, a more motley gathering it would have been hard to find anywhere. Some wore Boche overcoats, some their own, others had German top-boots on, and as none had had a shave or wash for days they looked the part of the " Terrible Australians."

Give the boys a few hours to themselves; and what a difference! By the following morning they looked as fresh as new pins; a shave, wash, and brush, on top of a good sleep, effect a wonderful transformation. The next day was also a rest in which there was time to elaborate the " possies " and incidentally reorganise the battalion after the heavy losses suffered on Sunday.

Twelve platoons were formed, four of twenty-seven other ranks and eight of twenty-one—in very truth a skeleton battalion. We had now made ourselves comfortable, and were quite prepared for, and fully expected, at least ten days in which to recuperate and train, but at 11.30 p.m. on the 4th orders were received for the battalion to be in readiness to move at an hour's notice. The whole camp immediately assumed an air of bustle and energy; stores had to be loaded; Lewis guns drawn, ammunition and bombs issued, and the transport brought up to the camp from Curlu. It was hardly necessary to add that no one was exactly delighted at the prospect of moving again; yet the wonderful spirit which had animated everyone throughout the preceding month enabled all preparations to be completed within the prescribed time.

However, there need have been no violent hurry, as we did not leave until the afternoon of the 5th. The reason for all this haste was that the Boche was falling back so rapidly that we were in danger of losing touch with him—news which went a long way towards consoling us for the loss of our much-needed rest. Leaving Cheesewood about four in the afternoon we travelled a road thickly crowded with transport, as everything that could move forward was doing so, and half of the way we were not able to keep to the road, but had to take to the fields to make any progress at all. On reaching the few ruins which had once been the village of Clery-sur-Somme, a halt was made for a meal. The cookers had gone ahead and everything was ready for us. It was rather an unfortunate position, as the sheds in the vicinity contained the decomposing carcases of some horses killed by shell-fire.

The meal had hardly begun when a heavy thunderstorm necessitated the wearing of ground-sheets and a rush to any shelter available among the ruins. By the time we were ready to start the road was absolutely blocked with traffic—guns of all calibres, and miles and miles of wagons and limbers; but taking to the fields again we struggled on over the ridge down into the valley through which runs the half-completed Canal du Nord, looking even more desolate owing to the devastation—shell-holes and wrecked bridges—wrought all along its course. In this valley six-inch howitzers were working at top speed, firing from the open without the slightest concealment. We followed the canal along, turning into the Bapaume-Peronne road over the ruins of a large arched bridge that spanned the canal-bed; thence on towards Mont. St. Quentin, halting just beyond the point where a railway crosses the road. All will remember here a small dump of " rubber gun " shells, and empty cases in plenty, evidently a " possie " from which some of the souvenirs we received at Cheesewood and Curlu had started on their journey. We camped for the night in the old trenches on the historic Mont. St. Quentin, one of the strongest natural positions one could wish to occupy. Abundance of enemy overcoats were to be obtained, and with these the battalion made themselves fairly comfortable.

At 3 a.m. the following morning everyone was astir and making tracks for the cookers, where a remarkably good meal was awaiting us. By 4 a.m. we were on the move again in battle-formation with transports in rear, the 43rd Battalion on our left, and the 44th on our right. With the 42nd Battalion and the 3rd Divisional Pioneers forming a vanguard, we felt quite secure, and the advance was more in the nature of a route-march than anything else.

The sun was just shining as we passed through the ruins of Mont. St. Quentin. These had the appearance of ruins of some bygone age rather than of but four years. It was difficult to realise that a modern village had ever stood here, where was only grass and a few moss-covered bricks. After leaving here we turned away from the roads and made across country in the direction of Bussu.

Here was every trace of recent encounters, but it was not until we were resting in a sunken road that we heard any hostile shells, and these were few, and far away to our left front. Continuing our advance in artillery formation and passing to the right of Bussu we took up positions in the vicinity of Buire Wood, a fair-sized wood on the crest of the hill across the valley from Bussu.

Battalion Headquarters was established at Cardinal Wood. We were now under slight artillery fire, but it was not serious. While waiting here, we had a visit from as impudent a Fritz airman as it would be possible to find. Flying exceedingly low, certainly not more than one hundred and fifty feet up, he first had a good look at our advancing troops, and then followed the valley down towards Peronne. "Archies," machine guns, and rifles were blazing away at him in good style, but apparently to no effect. While dodging our "Archies" this aviator dropped in our lines a map on which he had marked the positions of our troops and artillery, thus probably saving us considerable trouble, as he did not get a chance of repeating his manœuvres. After remaining in these positions for a few hours we were able to continue our advance owing to the 42nd's fine efforts. These new positions we maintained until it was time for us to relieve the 42nd as vanguard. This happened some time near midnight, and by 3 a.m. on the following morning (the 7th) we were in position, with the 44th on our right and the 231st British Brigade on our left. As no previous reconnaissance had been made the task was a difficult one. Indeed, to find a given platoon solely by a map reference, on a dark night, over ground you have never seen before, is a task of no mean order, and reflected the greatest credit on those specially concerned. The rather rare German helmet of shining patent leather could be picked up in good numbers above Bussu. These helmets belonged to the Prussian Guard Regiment, who had been put to flight and compelled to leave much gear behind them. Souvenir-hunters took advantage of the opportunity, and added these helmets to their already extensive collections.

Our job now was to capture the "blue line," which ran along the ridge behind Roisel to the village of Hervilly. We had a detachment of the 13th Light Horse working in front as scouts, while a few of them acted as gallopers, doing yeoman service as such, too; in fact, it was mainly owing to their untiring energy that communication was so splendidly kept up. It was a lovely summer day, and the countryside very unwarlike in appearance; no trenches, few shell-holes, and the woods in full leaf, not that stripped-naked appearance generally associated with battlefields. Although there was a fair amount of machine-gun fire, no stout opposition, in the sense we knew it, was encountered until coming in front of Roisel. The whole advance reminded one somewhat of the stunts at Assinghem, only there were not so many casualties. However, on the battalion reaching the outskirts of Roisel, Fritz made himself felt. At Roisel he had machine guns in plenty, and some of his batteries were firing over open sights at us; but we soon got into touch with our artillery, who immediately set to work and made the town such a lively place for a while, that, much as we would have liked to hurry Fritz out of the town, we were prevented by the heavy shell-fire from our own guns, which, having once started, seemed unwilling to "knock off." We were, therefore, compelled to flank the town, and "C" Company, making splendid progress, went round to the left of it, and by 8.30 a.m. had firmly established themselves in their new position. In the meantime the rest of the battalion, having captured the villages of Hamel, Marquaix, and Hamelet, were held up on the high ground to the south-west of Roisel, owing to the 44th on our right encountering heavy opposition, and as enemy machine guns enfiladed the gully running north to Roisel, both "A" and "B" companies had to wait until the right flank moved forward. Later in the afternoon the advance was continued on the right flank, the result being that by dusk Hervilly was taken and we were established along the whole of the blue line. Throughout this operation the enemy, when pressed, fell back without offering much resistance, consequently our losses were not heavy. Towards nightfall was the worst time, when, having a fair idea where we were, he made things rather lively, particularly for "A" and "B" Companies. It was fortunate for us that we gave Roisel a wide berth, as he simply poured heavy stuff (including 8-inch) into it after our artillery ceased, but apart from scattering bricks and mortar little damage was done. That day's operations most nearly resembled what we had expected warfare to be when we enlisted. It was not a battle in the ordinary sense, but a chase after an enemy who had little or no desire to meet us, and who only offered resistance when he was simply forced to, owing to our men going ahead so fast. Then, like a rat in a corner, he would turn; those who had no opportunity of "kamerading," and found themselves stilll alive, would be quickly on the run again. Our capture for the day included between sixty and seventy transport, one 5.9-inch howitzer, one 4.2-inch howitzer, ten machine guns, and a huge dump of material of all sorts in Roisel. Towards midnight we were relieved by the 10th Brigade, and by daylight we had reached our bivouac. These were old Nissen huts captured by Fritz in his March push, and were built on the slope of a large escarpment in a series of terraces in a valley running north from Tincourt. The next morning at 10.30 the whole battalion moved to rest-huts in a wood not far from Doingt, which were reached in time for lunch. The following day it rained heavily, and we soon found that shrapnel had riddled the huts sufficiently to let the water in, so that it was a case of setting-to and patching with what material we could find; at the same time we had to revet the huts to guard against enemy bombing. During the night Gothas visited us, but appeared to be after Peronne, three kilometres away, as it was down that direction that most of the bombs fell. Training, that bugbear of army life, started on the 11th, but it was only a two-hours-a-morning affair, so that there was no real cause for anyone to complain. Boche 'planes were very persistent every night during our stay here, but " our side " had a great win on the night of the 13th. After several alarms, most of us had at last put our beds down, when the unmistakeable drone of a Hun engine was heard. Searchlights shot up from all directions and picked the 'plane up at once—really marvellous work. " Archies " and machine guns were going strongly and, try as he might, the 'plane could not escape the fateful beam. Suddenly tracer-bullets were noticed pouring into the Boche machine, and amidst great cheering and whistling from the spectators in the surrounding countryside, down came the 'plane in flames, Verey lights of all colours bursting into flame on the way down. In a similar manner the searchlights quickly picked up three more bombers that night, and a British 'plane did the rest. From now on, our searchlights did splendid work, picking up 'planes immediately; whether the result of new methods or by mere luck it does not matter. Thus they kept the coast fairly clear, and enabled us to enjoy undisturbed sleep at night. Our stay in this camp was brightened considerably by cricket and football matches, and hardly a night passed without a concert. The " Coo-ees " were showing down on Doingt, and we had occasional impromptu concerts in the Y.M.C.A. Hut. One night, while the concert was in full swing, Fritz came over, and the old cry went up, " Lights out." Lights were no sooner out than the " All clear " was sounded, and the programme resumed. But it was no good—some had a suspicion that the R.S.M. was annoyed because he was not asked to sing, as he blew those lights " out " and " up " so often that they had to give the concert up. While we were here two Casualty Clearing Stations were erected close by—a good indication of the rapidity of the advance. The Brigade sports were held on the 21st, and were thoroughly enjoyed by one and all, the great feature being the numerous sideshows and comic turnouts. The " chef d'œuvre," however, was the Court of Inquiry and Injustice, run by the Ambulance. All the appanages of a real court were in evidence—from judge, barristers, and a large police force to a Black Maria (which had recently belonged to Fritz and had been captured in Roisel).

The idea was to try all and sundry officers for some of their ever-recurring offences. Imagine our Padre being charged with " refusing to argue," a well-known Major with " being caught smiling," and an A.P.M. with " being found wandering in the front line." The fine varied with the offence, the result being a very tidy sum for the Red Cross Society. Route-marches came into vogue again during our last week at this camp—a fair omen of something to follow; but, compared with some of the extremist pattern of past memories, they were very moderate. It was not long now before somebody heard that "Somebody else had heard someone say," &c., &c., and the hut-strategists were soon busy manufacturing "furphies"; the sectors we were to operate in differed greatly, but all agreed as to our objective—Berlin. Therefore, with all this preliminary discussion, we were fully prepared when official movement orders came along.

CHAPTER 6.

En Route Towards the Hindenburg Line.—The Quarry near Villers Faucon.—29th September, 1918, the Battalion's Last Battle Commences.—The Failure of the Yanks.—The Hun's Anti-Tank Methods.—Barbed Wire and Machine Gun Possies.—Taking of the Hindenburg Line.—The Canal Tunnel.—5th October, Final Good-bye to Fritz.—Train Journey from Peronne to Airaines.—Warlus.

The camp in the woods near Doingt was a good home, and we were sorry to leave, but, as the C.O. himself said, we must be prepared to carry on the work we had begun so successfully, and drive the Hun yet further back, even though our endurance might have to be put to greater test than heretofore. This time the famous Hindenburg Line was our goal, and although, of course, we did not know it then, this stunt was to be our last. On 27th September the battalion set out on the long approach-march, following the main route through Tincourt to Roisel. High up in the evening sky to the east, reflected against a dark band of clouds, there shone a portent of good omen, a veritable "Rising Sun" picked out in the rays of light. This celestial phenomenon lasted for some considerable time, like to a prophetic beacon, heralding a victorious issue to the conflict in which we were about to take part. The road was crowded with traffic, causing some difficulty in keeping touch throughout the battalion, as we had to advance in single file where the traffic was thickest.

From Roisel we turned off towards Villers Faucon, and were not sorry to arrive at our destination after about seventeen kilometres' march, even though it were only a burrow in the bank, which probably required enlarging. Back once more, amid the roar of our artillery we settled down in the usual way, the cookers providing a midnight tea, and all sorting themselves out into dugouts. The chief feature of this bivouac was the great mound, forming part of a quarry, which was afterwards used as the 11th Brigade signalling station. From one o.clock to 5 a.m. the enemy sent over mustard-gas shells, and we had to put on masks for a while, but, in spite of the heavy concentration of gas in the valley, there was only one casualty from this cause. The line in this sector was held by Americans, who were to make their first attack on the

Siegfried Line. We were to come on behind, pass through them, and consolidate farther on. From the very start the outlook was unsatisfactory, for when our officers and N.C.O.'s went forward to Benjamin Post in reconnaissance, very little information could be gleamed concerning the projected sphere of operations and the enemy's positions. It transpired that the Americans had only the very vaguest knowledge of their sector. All our officers agreed that the front line occupied by the Americans had been erroneously defined, and that, instead of holding the Guillemont Farm-Quennemont Farm system, their front line was really nearer the Cat Post-Benjamin Post sector. Naturally the American troops, being new to war—this was the first time " in " for most of them—were unable to give the reconnaissance party the information they, experienced men, would like to have received. For our justification it is necessary to say that this inexperience of the Yanks was mainly responsible for our partial failure to accomplish the task set us, which would have been possible only if the American troops worked according to schedule, which they did not. The 41st Battalion's task was as follows :—We were to be left-front battalion on the 11th Brigade, with the 44th on the right and 38th on the left, and were to exploit the success of the American Division in front of us from the " green line " to the " red line." To reach the " green line " we were to pass various points at certain prearranged times.

It was hoped to reach the famous Canal Tunnel by five minutes past ten. The first part of the advance was to be made in line of platoons, all deploying before the reaching the tunnel. Instructions were issued that the battalion was not to participate in the fight for the " green line," but was to reserve its energy for the exploitation beyond. To assist us, we had attached to us four tanks, two trench-mortars, four machine guns, and eight field artillery pieces. On arrival at the " green line " we were to take up defensive positions, and to wait further orders.

So much for our plans ; the fates willed otherwise. At 7.15 a.m. on the 29th, after enjoying a good night's rest, the battalion assembled near the quarry, and commenced the forward march, the plan being to reach at 9 o'clock the " brown line," where it was hoped to get into touch with the 38th Battalion on our left. The morning was misty, and a considerable amount of mustard-gas was still hanging about in the gully. All ranks went forward in characteristic fashion, for, though they were not to be the first " over the top," they had great confidence in the Yanks.

Our first impression of the progress of the attack was received when the battalion was nearing Benjamin Post trench-system. Enemy machine guns were very active, and progress was difficult. At this stage, as it was evident that all was not going well with the Americans, the Intelligence Officer was despatched to warn all Company Commanders that they must, on no account, become involved in the fight for the present. This message was delivered successfully.

On the battalion reaching the Ronssoy-Bellimont road, the enemy put down a fairly heavy and continuous artillery barrage on the trenches in Claymore Valley and the vicinity, and this, combined with the activity of his machine guns and snipers, made it impossible to advance according to plan. B.H.Q. was accordingly established in Little Benjamin trench, and the battalion, in touch throughout, and also with the flanks, lay up in all available cover awaiting further instructions.

Owing to the mist becoming denser, observation of the progress of the attack was impossible. Fritz's strafe was very severe, and it is marvellous that our casualties were not greater, when crossing the open country beyond the sunken road at Benjamin Post. Half an hour after the halt, the Americans began to come in in small groups, reporting that they had been checked at the Guillemont-Quennemont line with heavy casualties, and it was quite evident that they had become disorganised.

Brigade was immediately advised and instructions as to further action requested. The reply stated that the attack had gone well in the south, and it was presumed that the Americans had pushed through without "mopping up." Acting on this assumption the C.O. ordered out patrols to reconnoitre Fritz machine gun positions and snipers with a view to surrounding them and getting the battalion forward. But Fritz had the advantage of position, and kept up a brisk fire, causing many casualties in the battalion. Lieutenant M. J. Flannery's platoon advanced to Quennot Copse, and began to work along the trench towards the enemy, but was soon met with vigorous bombing resistance. The trench was also rendered impassable on account of heavy barbed wire obstacles. The battalion only moved about two hundred yards forward, the fire from machine guns and snipers proving too strong to overcome in daylight, without assistance from artillery. There were many brilliant individual exploits, which unfortunately met with little success, and almost invariably ended disastrously for those who had ventured out. One Lewis gunner climbed out of the trench, and, firing from the hip, swept the enemy machine-gun positions, only to fall a few moments later shot through the head by a sniper. Lieutenant Dodds met with a similar fate, while standing up on the parapet to urge his men forward. The casualties for the morning were very heavy—nine officers and sixty men. Among those who fell were Lieutenants Brewer and Lawson. The former will long be remembered as one of our most conscientious officers, who knew well the ways and wants of the "Digger," having been through the mill himself. Not a man in the old No. 5 Platoon, "B" Company, that did not rejoice when Sergeant Brewer received his commission at Ste. Marie Cappell, although his gain meant their loss, as he was then transferred to another company.

It was terribly unlucky to be " knocked out " in the last stunt, and yet some had to pay the price. It is regrettable that fine men like Lieutenants Brewer and Lawson should have been numbered amongst the slain. Lieutenant Lawson left his cover in a gallant attempt to save a wounded sergeant of his company, who was lying in an exposed position some fifty yards away. He was instantly killed by a big shell, which burst close to him.

Not only in this stunt, but during the whole advance since 8th August, the battalion sustained heavy losses as far as officers were concerned. The following are the names of those who were severely wounded during this period, and who eventually returned to Australia without being able to join the battalion again :—Captains H. Chumleigh, C. W. S. French, M.C., and P. F. Calow, M.C.; Lieutenants G. S. Armstrong, B. Jackson, F. E. Perroux, L. H. Rogers, H. J. Wiles, D.S.O., W. D. Clarke, A. James-Wallace, and S. L. Robinson, M.C. The last four were wounded in the attack on the Hindenburg Line.

On our left the 38th Battalion was faced with similar conditions, so it was decided to postpone our advance for a while. The enemy appeared to have taken every possible measure to deal with our tanks, and his efforts to knock them out when the attack opened met with complete success. A prisoner stated that his field battery had special orders to deal with tanks, and that 77 mm. guns, anti-tank rifles, and light trench-mortars in addition to machine guns using the armour-piercing bullets, were all employed in checking their advance. Many of them struck mines, and could be seen down in the valley below Benjamin Post standing derelict in a row—some eight or ten of them. During the afternoon, in accordance with the C.O.'s instructions, all stray Americans, numbering about a hundred, and having with them a one-pound gun, were mustered and sent up to swell the ranks of our battalion. While this was being done, the companies lay up in hastily-dug positions—shell-holes and so forth. That evening we occupied Trollope and Triangle trenches, Quennot Copse, and a small part of Guillemont trench, our left being obliged to remain at the " scarp " running near the small road which joined the Ronssoy road at Benjamin Post. At nightfall we were successful in penetrating Guillemont trench, where we accounted for several Huns and captured five machine guns. Our casualties at the close of the first day amounted to about nine officers and one hundred other ranks killed and wounded.

At a conference that night, it was decided to attempt the capture of the whole system next morning. The 9th Brigade now took over the sector. At daybreak on the 30th the battalion moved forward, and occupied the more advanced positions overlooking the Hindenburg Line and Canal Tunnel. The only resistance was machine-gun fire at a long range. We increased our captures this morning to the extent of twenty-eight machine guns, one " Whizz-bang " gun, and an anti-tank rifle, besides a great number of rifles and two Lewis guns which the enemy had been using against us. Most of these captures were despatched to the War Museum.

After the battalion had been reorganised we occupied a line from Stave trench to Paul trench, including Quennemont Farm, while one company held Guillemont trench. Thus we remained for the next two days in reserve to the 9th Brigade, who went forward towards Le Catelet and Gouy, as far as the road running up Dirk Valley. The nights were chilly, but luckily the rain held off well, after the few showers which caused some discomfort during the first night.

The Americans suffered very heavy casualties, which seemed disproportionately great owing to the strength of their brigade. Everywhere one came across their bodies, and the stretcher-bearers were continually bringing in their wounded, many of whom had had their thighs shattered by anti-tank bullets.

The American failure to complete their task is attributed to the inexperience of all ranks, almost total loss of officers and N.C.O.'s, and appalling casualties sustained—all heavy factors in bringing about complete disorganisation. Men were to be found in every direction hopelessly lost, their gear abandoned, and much of this stuff, together with that left by their dead and wounded, found its way into the possession of the " Digger," only to be handed in when regulation compelled it.

No one questions the bravery of the individual Yank; this realisation and the apologies of the survivors did away with much of the keenness of our disappointment at our being unable for the first time to accomplish what we had set out to do, owing to the reasons beforementioned. The fact that the Americans' failure was so long in being realised by us did much to delay our progress, and we could not get artillery to work in support owing to the probable presence of American troops in front.

Anyhow, the fact remained that the Hindenburg Line—Fritz's last stronghold, one might say, in France—had been taken, and not only at this point but throughout its entire length.

There is no doubt that if he had been able to defend this particular line as strongly as the French held on to Verdun, we should have been checked for a considerable time, and could have only broken through after enormous casualties. The Hindenburg Line was not quite like what we expected. There were perfect mazes of wire, of course, and of tremendous depth, but the trench-system itself was not a great concrete fortress extending for miles and miles, as we had imagined. In this sector the trenches were very wide, but not well revetted, so that they had fallen away in places. Their blockhouses and machine-gun emplacements were well fortified and placed in the most advantageous positions. The dugouts being German, naturally left nothing to be desired. Behind his line, Fritz had the great Canal Tunnel, which he converted into one enormous dugout or underground barracks, connected by sloping shafts with his trench-system. One part of this must have been a huge kitchen, but a shell had messed things up considerably, and, perhaps, was the direct cause of a rumour which got about that down there the Hun carried on his diabolical scheme of boiling down his dead to obtain fat. Everybody will remember the thrill of horror caused by certain articles in the daily papers on this matter a year or so previous to this. One man said that he actually saw a portion of human flesh in a great cauldron already on the fire. What part the shell played in all this, of course we shall never know. On the first two days of October we remained in our positions littled troubled by shell-fire (which was directed on to cross-roads mainly), and practically immune from enemy aircraft. Our airmen had absolute command in the air, and easily outnumbered Fritz by three to one in all this advance. On the evening of the 2nd, the battalion was relieved, and returned to bivouacs near the Quarry, towards Villers Faucon, and the following morning started on the march back, an occasional long-range shell, whistling overhead, being the last souvenir of Fritz. It must be remembered that the war was by no means over then, and we fully expected, after a rest of a few weeks—if so long—we should be up in the line "boxing-on" once more. It seemed they could not do without us. Nevertheless, this was actually our last fight, and surely one could hardly imagine a more appropriate time for the curtain to fall upon the glorious "drama" of the 41st, under fire, than this, with the scene set at the Hindenburg Line, and our battalion, with the 9th Brigade, victoriously astride the great stronghold that the Hun had deemed impregnable.

As we left the scene of our last combat, we could look back over nearly two years of active service in France, with a feeling of honourable pride for all that the 41st had done, and with the knowledge that we held what must be an almost unequalled record, in that no member of the battalion had ever fallen into the clutches of the Boche.

The 41st Casualty Lists showed "No Prisoners."

For the march back the day turned out bright and sunny, and everyone felt light-hearted, looking forward to a good rest, probably in the " Bock Area " ; for, with a thirty-mile trail of devastation and ruins behind us, " BOCK " and " BACK " were no longer synonymous terms.

Soon after dinner we reached our destination in a valley about a mile from Aizecourt, near the Peronne-Cambrai road. Shelters were speedily erected, and the battalion settled down for a day or two. Near the camp was the damaged mounting of a great German howitzer. A " Woodbine " Labour Company occupied tents in the same valley. The 5th October will be remembered as an important date in our calendar. On that date we left the forward war-area for good and all, though nobody thought so at the time, and entrained for Peronne by light railway, following the road for a few miles. That was our last glimpse of the ruins of the ancient and historic town as we marched down the " ROO de KANGA " to the railway station. Company after company of American troops passed us, making their way towards the front as eager to get at Fritz and make a name for themselves as we were to get away for our well-earned rest.

While waiting for our " Train de Luxe " at Peronne (" Hauptbahn Hof " as the wretched Huns had labelled it), we had the satisfaction of seeing some of the fruits of our recent victories, the first batch of repatriated civilians returning down the line, coming home at last.

The train journey was most interesting to us. We passed through all that devastated belt of country which lies between Peronne and Amiens, Chaulnes, Rosieres, and then Villers Bretonneux, still vivid in our memory, and one had visions of 5.9's crashing into the town ; one could almost scent the poison-gas, and hear the ping-ping, rat-a-tat-tat of whizzing bullets, as the train rattled along down through the deep cutting, over which some of us had peered out into the darkness a few months earlier, with bombs ready at hand to hurl down upon the Hun, should he be so bold as to attack us by this road. But now all was tranquil, the bent and twisted rails had been relaid and holes filled in, and we were actually speeding in a railway train through that once bullet-swept cutting.

A few civilians were already back in this district, and so long had we been away in the desert of ruins and shell-holes, that the first sight of children playing and farmers working in the fields we had fought over called forth exclamations of satisfaction from all sides.

The country was now very familiar to us, and we picked out the old landmarks, the towers of Corbie, the "brickstack," and Glisy's slender spire, as we descended into the Somme Valley, and then a few minutes later our train steamed into that ancient city, between which and the German hordes we had dug ourselves in during the latter days of March, barring the last great bid for Paris and the coast—Amiens, queen city of the Somme, awaking at last from War's fell nightmare. Airaines, some thirty kilometres from Amiens, was the point where we detrained, and we marched out to the village of Warlus, four and a-half kilometres distant. It was growing dusk as we left Airaines and set out along the main Paris road, one of those long straight avenues which seem to stretch away into eternity.

WARLUS.

PHASE IX.

CHAPTER 1.

"Warlus Billets."—Civilisation Once More.—The "Prussian Guards."—The Band.—Training, Football and Sports.—Autumn Tints.—"Big Feeds."—Concerts.—11th November, the Armistice.—St. Maxent.—Christmas, 1918.—New Year, 1919.

Civilization ! That was the word uppermost in our thoughts as we settled into our billets in the barns and cottages at Warlus, a typical Somme village composed of mud walls, manure-heaps and duckponds, which seemed to us war-weary troops like a corner of Heaven, until the aftermath of French beer and "Vin Blong" brought speedy disillusion.

Now that we were definitely out for a spell of some duration, a comprehensive training syllabus was drawn up, leaving the afternoons open for sports of all kinds, and an all-round smartening up of the battalion commenced, which eventually gained for us considerable fame ; in fact, we soon came to be known as the "Prussian Guards." One of the outstanding features of the training syllabus was the daily march round after the battalion-parade in the morning, with bayonets fixed and the band playing "Blaze Away." That particular march tune will always bring back to our minds the "mad mile" of those Warlus days. A "Dinkum" Guard, too, magnificently groomed and polished, mounted daily at Headquarters—the school yard—to the strains of the brass band.

On the 17th October Brigadier-General Cannan inspected the whole battalion, and the subsequent report on the turnout was distinctly satisfactory. It was soon after this that the long-expected amalgamation of the 41st and 42nd Battalions took place. The remnant of the 42nd that joined us on the 23rd formed a new "B" Company, thus bringing the battalion strength up to four companies once more. Headquarters had now also been formed into a company with personnel and establishment like the rest.

The parade on the 24th was, therefore, an historical one, being the first appearance of the two sister battalions on the parade ground, forming together a new 41st. It seemed hard on the 42nd, to be thus broken up at the eleventh hour, after having won such renown during the past two years, with the Hamel stunt and many glorious deeds to their credit, more especially at this time, when the war was nearly over. Bulgaria had already given in, and Turkey and Austria were on the verge of surrender. With the 42nd came the Pipers, who startled all the villagers of Warlus the first morning after their arrival with weird music from the "Hielan's," and henceforth contributed their quota to the rather extensive musical programme, which had now become part of the daily routine. Our brass band welcomed this timely relief, and later, after their return from Le Treport, the 42nd brass band was incorporated with them. The 41st band was unfortunate with sergeant-conductors. When Sergeant Rickards wielded the baton, we enjoyed some splendid programmes, and new pieces and selections were surprising us almost daily, when he had to leave the battalion, being invalided back to Australia. But a worthy successor was found in Corporal Murray, who was later appointed Band-Sergeant, and he carried on the good work that Rickards had commenced, bringing the 41st band to a pitch of excellence that put many another battalion band in the shade, and made route-marches almost enjoyable at times with the increased snap and vigour of their performances. And then just as everything was going swimmingly, Sergeant Murray fell a victim to the all-prevailing "Flu," and Sergeant Phillips, our versatile friend from the Battalion Orderly-room, took over, assisted by the regimental composer, Private Vesperman, whose marches and waltzes are now well known. The days at Warlus slipped by quickly enough with the usual routine, and when the 1st Divisional Artillery moved out of Airaines on its way up to the front, rumours were prevalent that we would have to follow suit very shortly, although, when Austria "threw in the towel," hopes ran high that we might not be required after all ; nor were we disappointed, for Germany, now deserted by her Allies, and hemmed in on all sides by the British Naval Blockade, with her harassed army falling back all along the line before Foch's incessant blows, was compelled at last to ask for an armistice. This unconditional surrender—the terms of the armistice were such that the signing of it meant nothing more nor less than that—is now a matter of history, and the 11th November, a date which will rank henceforth as the most glorious festival in the calendar, the ever-memorable day when the greatest war in the world's history virtually came to an end. In our little out-of-the-way village there were no visible signs of rejoicing, and no official information was sent to the battalion on that day, although all the French people in the district knew full well that the armistice had been signed, and that "la guerre" was "napoo," and wondered why we still carried on as though nothing unusual had happened. However, the victory was duly celebrated in the estaminets in the usual way, and everyone felt as if a great weight had been suddenly lifted from his mind. Never again would we hear the nerve-racking shriek and crash of shells, nor stand for days shivering in the mud of the trenches ; never again would the Gothas disturb our slumbers with their drone, and rain death upon us from the sky. Now it was that we looked back over those last months of hard fighting with a feeling of thankfulness that we had come through safely, at the same time remembering our "Cobbers" who had fallen, especially those who had the supreme misfortune of being knocked in the last stunt. And now, too, Australia drew appreciably nearer. Next year, at any rate, we ought to be at home.

With Armistice-day, a suitable time is found to bring this brief history to an end. It came in November, which continued for a while the delightful weather of October, when the woods were changing from summer green to the red and gold of their autumn splendour. After the visions of shell-blasted stumps, that had passed for woods in the battle area, the beauties of this, our last autumn in France, struck us all the more forcibly. As the battalion was unable to return to Australia as a complete unit, the five months or so which elapsed before the first draft left England are not of particular interest, being occupied mostly in filling-in forms of variegated colours, attending lectures under the Educational Scheme and playing football, when weather permitted. One might mention however, our stay in "Venice" or rather St. Maxent, near Abbeville. It needs no description; it was truly Venetian—that is to say, the waterways were there without the picturesque setting. Thanks to Lieutenant Tardent's drainage scheme, Headquarters Company Orderly-room could eventually be approached from both sides by non-swimmers. Soon after our arrival someone aptly remarked, "Where the H——— is the harbour-master of this ——— village?"

There is also a story that a man was late for parade one day, and on being asked the reason replied, "Some blighter pinched my dinghy."

Meanwhile, Christmas came and went, the first real "peace and goodwill" Christmas for years, bringing on this account a more than usual amount of good fare and jollity. Very wet and stormy weather ushered in the New Year, 1919; the glorious year which was destined to bring us our heart's desire—a triumphant and safe return home to AUSTRALIA, there as citizens, each with the consciousness of having "done his bit" for his country, to settle down in the fulness of time to a more serious and better life than we had passed through during the years of the GREAT WAR.

Roll of Members of the 41st Battalion.

Adam, R. R. J. (M.M.)
Abbott, W. J.
Ahbol, L. E.
Ackerman, L.
Armstrong, W.
Ah See, W.
Akers, F. J.
Austin, W.
Allan, H.
Ashwood, E. (M.M.)
Ayre, W. J.
Austin, R. H.
Archer, F.
Allison, W. J.
Allison, C. C.
Anderson, C. A. Mc.
Ashton, E. D. (M.M.)
Anderson, D. M.
Allan, J.
Anderson, A. A.
Arthur, A. V.
Anderson, H. H.
Ault, A. H.
Allison, R.
Ashwood, F. G.
Aris, B. W.
Aitkins, A. J.
Arnold, G.
Alward, M.
Abbott, F. W.
Anderson, A. P.
Andrews, J. J.
Andrews, W. W.
Avery, R. E.
Ansell, C. J. (M.M.)
Askew, J. T.
Allanson, S. A. H.
Ashby, W. G.
Ashburn, R. G.
Attwell, H. F.
Alshorn, M.
Addison, W. J.
Allen, T.
Anderson, S. M.
Andrews, T. E.
Adams, J.
Andrews, F. G. W.
Anderson, T. J.
Anderson, E.
Armstrong, R. J. T. (M.M.)
Adams, S. H.
Anderson, G. A.
Alley, G. K.
Atkinson, F. D.
Alwyne, H.
Albrand, H. G.

Adams, A. H.
Addison, J.
Amos, C. P.
Appleby, I. K.
Astill, J.
Adams, B. J.
Attridge, F. H.
Allan, J. T.
Ayers, A.
Armstrong, P.
Arnold, A. E. J.
Anderson, A.
Alexander, T. H.
Austin, F. S.
Atkinson, W. B.
Anderson, A. A.
Arthur, A. V.
Aitken, J. C.
Aspinall, A. H. L.
Adams, J.
Alexander, C. D.
Archbold, W. J.
Allen, W. H.
Arnold, C. H.
Aitken, A.
Adams, A. B.
Armstrong, G.
Allan, J.
Aaskob, A. H.
Anderson, Capt. L. W. C.
Adair, Lieut. A. P. H.
Armstrong, Lieut. G. S.
Asche, Lieut. F. S.
Armstrong, Lieut. G. D.
Argue, Lieut. R. W.

Blackshaw, H. A.
Bennett, A.
Birgan, B.
Barnes, W.
Baxter, G.
Blakey, W. S.
Burrows, S. E. T.
Byth, A.
Belford, C. G.
Box, G. A.
Byrne, J. G.
Brown, D.
Baumgartner, J.
Bletcher, V. R.
Bailey, C. R.
Bretherton, R. D.
Baker, G.
Browning, A.
Brookes, A. H.

Baxter, T. H.
Brown, E. B.
Bowdery, A. G.
Brenchley, G. W.
Bingham, R.
Bryson, A.
Brosnan, T. M.
Bertling, A. E. L.
Brandt, A.
Bilston, O. T. L. A.
Buttenshaw, F. J.
Brownsey, O. E.
Buchan, A.
Butler, T. T.
Browning, H.
Bimrose, G. R.
Barryman, T. L.
Byrnes, P. A.
Brown, H. J.
Beitz, W. F.
Bloom, E.
Brewer, Lieut. R.
Bowen, W. R.
Bull, E. J.
Burke, T. W.
Bird, T.
Brown, R.
Baker, A. V.
Browning, D.
Brown, F.
Brown, C. A.
Bennett, S. C.
Boland, R.
Brooke, S.
Bennett, J.
Bunn, E.
Bastick, W. H. C.
Beresford, C.
Bonser, A.
Boyle, A. H.
Burnett, G. O.
Barker, S. T.
Bustin, T. M.
Bahr, F. E.
Barker, R. W.
Briskey, W. C. (M.M.)
Benson, W. R.
Boyce, L. H.
Boyce, L. A. G.
Brighton, F.
Burns, W. C.
Beal, D. F.
Bailey, G.
Buzza, D. W.
Bow, A.
Breen, A. J. (D.C.M.)

Bramley, A. A.
Bell, J. P.
Baker, G.
Bellingham, T.
Bell, M. J.
Beetham, C.
Brooks, P.
Barrie, J.
Barrie, T. F.
Broom, J. A.
Bell, J. J.
Bates, G.
Burns, F.
Brown, A.
Bavister, J. T.
Barclay, J. B.
Byrnes, E. J.
Bentham, W.
Blandford, C. V.
Beattie, F.
Bailey, R. J.
Baillie, C. L.
Baxter, J. L.
Bruce, S.
Brown, T. E.
Barker, P.
Bartrim, A. J.
Bates, A.
Bryant, R. J. (M.M.)
Burrows, J. E.
Brown, W. J.
Bartlett, J.
Brownlie, W. R.
Bamsey, P. E.
Barker, F. G.
Brown, G. A. H.
Beggs, L. C.
Blayney, W.
Blinman, H.
Butler, C.
Blanch, J. B. C.
Barnett, F. W.
Brown, H. H.
Bashforth, G. T.
Burke, J. P.
Beamish, H. W.
Bett, J. R.
Begley, J. P.
Boyce, L. F.
Bullock, L. J.
Binnington, J.
Burnett, R. W.
Bell, G.
Bevis, H.
Brown, D. H.
Beech, W. T.

Boyle, F.
Belcher, L. R.
Brown, N. W.
Bently, R.
Butler, C. F. (M.M.)
Bagnall, W.
Brandt, A.
Bathe, A. A.
Berry, E. C.
Berry, J. W.
Britcher, W.
Bennett, G. R.
Bright, J. F.
Brennan, J.
Booth, W.
Bennett, T.
Brewer, E.
Brebner, J. K.
Brittain, W. S. G.
Birkett, F. D.
Barton, G. H.
Birkett, G. V.
Bryant, W. J.
Bezant, H. J.
Bond, A.
Bryant, F. G.
Beattie, H. W.
Bourne, R. G.
Booth, J. R.
Boyle, G.
Boutle, L. R.
Battley, W.
Berthlesen, H. W.
Balloch, J.
Butler, D. T.
Blackman, A. J.
Blackman, T.
Bird, R. A.
Brookman, F.
Brownlie, W. R.
Brent, G.
Burns, F. N.
Bourke, J. T.
Barber, H. K.
Byrnes, A. H.
Bower, R.
Blanchett, R. C.
Bell, H.
Blair, W. M.
Bint, F. C.
Burns, G. H. H.
Born, A. W.
Bertram, F. D.
Bertram, P. St. A.
Bax, W. J.
Bergveld, J. G. F.
Bates, F. S.
Brady, E. P.
Biegel, J. T. D.
Buckney, A. J.
Bird, E. A.
Brown, W. C. (M.M.)
Boulton, G. O.
Briggs, C.

Bahr, W.
Beddoes, T. A.
Burrows, W. R. V.
Barclay, R.
Barbour, J.
Bailey, A. G.
Bradfield, C. A.
Bauer, W. A.
Boase, G. B.
Barnes, T.
Bryce, J. J.
Bailes, J. J.
Brown, G.
Brooks, G. W.
Bojack, J. F. A.
Barnes, E. W.
Baker, G.
Browning, F. E.
Bruce, E.
Blackbell, J.
Brecknell, F. W.
Barnes, F. C.
Bamberry, A. J.
Barnett, E. J.
Bean, F.
Barnett, D.
Binns, W.
Brown, G.
Bale, G. A.
Berry, J. W.
Boneham, R.
Brown, W. H.
Burgess, T.
Box, P. A.
Brown, A.
Biggs, P. J.
Brooks, G.
Bell, W. J.
Budd, W. J.
Burgess, W. H.
Beggs, L. C.
Brown, A.
Beckman, A.
Beck, A.
Borgstahl, W.
Branson, C. H.
Billett, A.
Benstead, A. E.
Beresford, N. G.
Baker, C. H. V.
Benthe, H. C.
Belcher, G.
Bremner, A. G.
Brooks, O. V.
Baker, H.
Buckby, N.
Belcher, E. S. K.
Bourke, E. J.
Bartlam, A. R. Y.
Bardwell, H. W.
Brannigan, H.
Butler, J. A.
Burton, C. B.
Burton, G.

Batston, G. P.
Boyle, H. P. (M.M.)
Bennett, A.
Buchan, T. H.
Baynes, J. H.
Borger, J. H.
Bigg, W. A.
Brennan, H.
Ball, W. J.
Beattie, W.
Borgen, V. A.
Bodger, H. A.
Brigham, G. H.
Burgess, T.
Button, M. G. B.
Beeston, F. A.
Bradford, C. H.
Brown, A. W.
Board, Lieut.-Col. F. J.
Brown, Lieut. A. J.
Boyce, Lieut. L. A. G. (M.C.)
Brown, Lieut. D. (M.C.)
Broadfoot, Lieut. C. J.
Byrne, Lieut. E. H.
Butler, Lieut. C. H. (M.C. & Bar)
Baxter, Lieut. G.
Burtenshaw, Lieut. F. J. (M.C.)
Broom, Lieut. G. V. M.
Burnett, Lieut. G. O. (M.M.)

Chalk, J. T.
Cahill, C.
Conroy, E. J.
Clark, L.
Chadwick, C. C.
Croft, E.
Campbell, M. J.
Cooper, E. R.
Chapman, W.
Conn, R. C.
Cock, W. H.
Collins, J. L.
Curtis, E.
Cook, A.
Culluc, W.
Chardon, N. F.
Campbell, T. H.
Chasser, A. R.
Clifford, W. J.
Cowlrich, S.
Collett, R. F.
Crook, G. S.
Cowan, A. J.
Casey, A. G.
Clayton, W.
Clancy, S.
Cowen, T. J.
Curtis, C. H.
Curtis, G.
Cooney, P.
Childs, H. J.

Carson, W.
Collins, H.
Chandler, E. J.
Collins, J.
Cobb, T.
Cathcart, D.
Cleland, G. R. (M.M.)
Clarke, A. C.
Cummings, J. M.
Chalk, R. B.
Cooke, J. C.
Cowley, S. W.
Coulter, E. S.
Crawford, S. F.
Croft, E.
Coste, M.
Cranney, T.
Collins, S. L.
Cook, H.
Campbell, J.
Cummings, A. E.
Coward, G. B.
Cohen, M. C.
Cumiskey, F. J.
Campbell, J. D.
Camerilli, B.
Crook, H.
Cross, W. E.
Clemo, J. R.
Clohessy, M. J.
Cornwall, J. A.
Carter, J. L.
Cane, M. P.
Clarke-Kennedy, H.
Conroy, L. F.
Cameron, H. A.
Clark, J.
Chumleigh, Capt. H.
Cassidy, Lieut J. J.
Clark, F. L. R.
Clarke, C. E.
Crombie, L. J.
Cottrell, H. J.
Clarke, N. W.
Carlson, C. (D.C.M.)
Coughlin, H. E.
Cripps, B. A.
Cole, C. F.
Cudday, L. (M.M.)
Colville, Lieut. F. A.
Carroll, W. J.
Clews, J. S. B.
Culluc, G. L. (M.M.)
Cowap, W. H.
Clarke, J.
Crossley, W.
Caldwell, S.
Carkeet, P. H.
Cottle, F.
Chevally, A.
Cahill, J. S.
Clark, J.
Carter, S. H.
Cooke, E. A.

Coe, L.
Couch, P. J.
Cooper, T. G.
Carroll, J.
Carr, A. C.
Catten, C. J.
Clarke, W.
Costello, B. W. (M.M.)
Craig, J.
Cliffe, S.
Cockburn, E.
Collins, P. C. G.
Crawford, M. E.
Cleland, E.
Campbell, J.
Catchpole, A. H.
Crossley, W. F.
Cantwell, J. J.
Cokely, D.
Clarke, J.
Clarke, G. T.
Campbell, A. G.
Crawford, E. G.
Cousins, W. A.
Coney, T.
Crowther, L. J.
Cahill, T. H.
Callanan, M.
Carrington, G.
Chadwick, W. J.
Crawford, R.
Collins, S.
Chaplin, C. E.
Crean, G.
Callaghan, E. W.
Campbell, C. S.
Conway, O. W.
Chellingworth, J.
Coleman, T.
Cripps, Lieut. B. A.
Colebach, H. G.
Carroll, W.
Cole, L. V.
Crail, Lieut. H.
Court, R. G.
Carter, H. G.
Clayworth, T. H.
Claydon, A. W.
Cudday, F. H. G.
Carstens, C. N.
Calder, T. S.
Chalmers, W.
Cleland, R. G.
Campbell, M. W.
Curtis, B.
Cummins, W. D.
Carroll, H. R.
Crowe, J. J.
Campbell, O. R.
Cottell, H. V.
Cross, T.
Cook, W.
Cooper, A. J.
Cupples, B. A.

Carter, W. J.
Chapman, E. G.
Cousin, J. E.
Carr, C.
Cottle, W. H.
Clay, H. J.
Clark, C.
Carter, A. B.
Cash, J. S.
Caless, G. R.
Cardew, Lieut. L.
Crocombe, A. G.
Carroll, P. C.
Close, H. J.
Casey, P. P.
Connor, C. E.
Cherry, H. E.
Christianson, C. C.
Casey, J. R.
Chadwick, T.
Collins, P. W.
Cleary, J.
Cox, W. L. (M.M.)
Cunningham, C. B.
Carrie, J.
Campbell, J. A.
Currey, R. W.
Curtis, H.
Connell, V.
Cheffins, F.
Cormack, D.
Cameron, D. G.
Card, T.
Christensen, A.
Chandler, H.
Conway, J. H.
Caven, C.
Cope, G. E.
Clark, J. G. A.
Curtis, A.
Carrigg, A. G.
Crawford, R.
Cavey, G.
Cornford, C. A.
Christoe, Major J. E.
Clark, Lieut. W. D.
Cobb, Lieut. H. L.
Calow, Capt. P. F. (M.C.)
Campbell, Lieut. R. C.
Coulthard, F.
Craig, G. M.
Coe, J.
Coyle, E. T.
Conn, J. H.
Campbell, P. B.
Claridge, O. A. J.
Cullen, J. P.
Cousin, A. M.
Cummins, T. P.
Cox, A. T.
Coppins, W.
Collins, A. C.
Camp, F. E.
Charles, J. H.

Cunningham, D. P.
Cawley, T. W.
Cooke, S. R.
Carmichael, H.
Crawford, C. M.
Campbell, A. G.
Clarkson, J. D.
Cozens, J. D.
Cole, G. M.
Clarke, H. L.
Cameron, G. C.
Colbert, J. E.
Cunningham, A. M.
Costello, M.
Crossley, E.
Counsell, C.
Cowan, A. J. R.
Cantwell, M. E.
Cook, E. W. (M.M.)
Crombie, J.
Carter, T. (M.M.)
Curtis, E.
Clare, C. M.
Chittick, H.
Currie, D.
Colsell, H.
Clydesdale, D. K.
Court, W. J.
Corbett, S.
Carr-Boyd, W. H.
Cooper, A. W.
Cross, T.
Cavell, W. J.
Cretney, T. H.
Cooper, J. W.
Cavendish, H.
Clark, J.

Douglas, Lieut. R. C. S.
Daly, P. J.
Donaldson, A. C.
Donaldson, J. F.
Dodd, C. J. W.
Dell, T. H.
Duncan, J.
Davidson, J.
Dempster, J.
Dixon, V.
Davies, O. M.
Donaldson, A.
Dodds, T. R.
Dale, H. H.
Dunlop, W. H.
Dummer, Lieut. L. S.
Dodd, H. H. (M.M.)
Duncan, W. G.
Dodds, A. E.
Dean, J. A. (D.C.M.)
Dick, J. R. (M.M.)
Duckworth, H. G.
Day, F.
Dougherty, C. A.
Dunn, H. W.

Doig, D. P.
Drylie, R.
Dines, W. C.
Donald, T.
Duggan, W.
Doig, H. G. A.
Dohenny, J. C.
Delacour, P. J.
Dale, R. G.
Dwyer, J. J. (MM.)
Dyer, G. F.
De St. Hilaire, R. A.
Davey, C. A.
Downton, G.
Day, C. W.
Duley, E. W.
Durrington, O. S.
Davey, G.
Davis, J. R.
Dunsford, A. G. (M.M.)
Dale, E. T.
Daniel, A. F.
Dykes, G. P.
Deeves, C. H.
Duffy, E. C.
Durrington, A. A. (M.M.)
Davies, F. A.
Dixon, E. (D.C.M., M.M.)
Dumbrell, W. W.
Durbin, G. A.
Davis, W. E.
Davies, E. J.
Dann, C. A.
Dun, J. C. (D.C.M.)
Dennis, H.
Duffy, R. W.
Duffy, A.
Dougherty, V.
Duncan, W.
Drew, H. E.
Downward, W. J.
Dunn, J.
Duncan, J. M.
Dodds, Lieut. G. S.
Dark, W. H.
Dwyer, E. E.
Dibdin, Major E. J. (D.S.O.)
Dinnie, Lieut. R. D.
Daw, J. K.
Dean, E. E.
De Raeve, E. U.
Dyson, T.
Dobson, J. R.
Dougherty, E. M.
Dean, L. H.
Doughley, S. R.
Daniel, E.
Dicker, G.
Dickson, J. H.
Daly, J. H.
Duggan, K. E.
Duff, D.
Dwyer, F. L.
Daly, L. J.

Dagg, R. E.
Doughlass, H.
Dallis, A. E.
Dicker, G.
Davies, H. M.
Duncan, J. A.
Doyle, E. L.
Drabsch, R. A.
Day, E.
Day, R. W.
Dale, E. T.
Dance, E. E.
Dawson, W.
Danke, T.
Dombrow, E. O.
Davies, G. S.
Davies, A. D.
Dean, T.
Duce, G. J.
Davies, W. G.
Dean, T. R.
Duffy, E.
Dockery, J.
Dalton, W. F.
Dewsberry, W. A.
Dennis, W. H.
Devery, D.
Duffett, W. I. M.
Doyle, D.
Donnelly, J. T.
Dearlove, A.
Draddy, J. T. P.
Dunn, N. S.
De Broughe, A. J.
Donahoo, J. A.
Dwyer, E. J.
Davies, O. C.
Douglass, J.
Day, W. C.
Day, T. G.
Davidson, G.
Davis, E. A.
Dixon, J. E.
Donaldson, H. W. R.
Dippy, A.
Davidson, A. M.
Day, E. A.
Drew, S. J.
Duncan, R.
Doyle, C. J.
Davies, H.
Downs, S. H.
Donald, Capt. D. G. E.
Dickie, Lieut. A.
Dimmock, Lieut. A. E.

Earnshaw, W. A.
Edge, E.
Earley, W. G.
Elliott, W. T.
Erskine, W. H.
Elms, B. G.
Edwards, J. R.

Eccles, A. E.
Evans, E. L.
Ellem, B. A.
Edwards, A. (D.C.M.)
Ellis, C. B. (M.M.)
England, H.
Egglestaff, V. G.
Evans, A. A. A.
Eggins, P.
Ellis, R. R.
Eustace, W.
Ellem, T. H.
Ellem, A. R.
Ellem, W. A.
Ellis, A.
Epps, R. H.
Ellem, A. J.
Egan, M.
Ekeberg, R. F.
Eaton, R.
Eagleton, J.
Ellis, R. W.
Evans, H.
Ellis, R. M.
East, G. T.
Edwards, I. T.
Evans, H. J.
Eltham, F.
Edwards, T. R. P.
Exton, W. T.
Edwards, E.
Edwards, T. H.
Eising, W. F.
Eales, H. J.
Ellis, J. H.
Eisentrager, F.
Elworthy, R.
Engels, F. G.
Exton, W.
Enright, J. T.
Eastwell, C.
Eardley, M. W.
Elder, R. P.
Eager, T.
Evans, W. A.
Edwards, J. E.
Epps, J. H.

Forrest, J.
Foo, J.
Fitzgerald, L. G.
Fitzner, C. F.
Forsyth, H.
Fairley, W. E.
Forbes, W.
Francis, A. V. E.
Fraser, W. A.
Friend, R. A. S.
Ford, G.
Fitchew, F. H.
Finn, P.
Freeman, G.
Fellows, S. A.

Follington, T. D. (M.M.)
Follington, C. S.
Findlay, J. G.
Foster, H.
Fraser, A.
Fibbins, A.
Fitch, B.
Fraser, B.
Fisher, S. E.
Fisher, I.
Fisher, G.
Fuller, T. G. (M.M.)
Flynn, J. T.
Ford, W.
Fogg, G. H.
Fleming, T. W.
Fisher, P. C.
Finger, F. H.
Fitzsimmons, O. J.
Fox, O. J.
Freeman, O. C.
Fraser, J. A.
Freshwater, A. J.
Freemantle, A.
Ferguson, J.
Funnell, G.
Fitzgerald, M.
Faulkner, S. F.
Frederickson, R. M. (M.M.)
French, G. H.
Fitzgerald, T.
Fawcett, W. H.
Fitzgerald, J. J.
Ferguson, J. M. (M.S.M.)
Fitzgerald, T. (M.M.)
Ferris, F.
Foy, C.
Flowers, J. B. R.
Fricker, C. F.
Ford, W.
Flynn, M. T.
Fairfull, J.
Fletcher, J. F.
Fagg, C. G.
Falvey, E.
Fahey, W.
Fraser, W.
Franklin, H.
Forsyth, W. J. (M.M.)
Farrelly, S. P.
Fudge, T. R.
Ford, D. H.
Fell, G. R.
Fredericksen, H. C.
Fredericks, H.
Fyles, E. A.
Francis, W. M.
Fraser, A. A.
Ferrari, J.
Fordshaw, R.
Fletcher, L. P.
Foster, C.
Fitzgerald, E.
Ferguson, A. G.

Freeman, A.
Fabrey, W.
Freeman, A. G.
Fullerton, R.
Fraser, D. McQ.
Furness, W. B.
Fisher, T.
Forsyth, N. A.
Fagg, C. G.
Fernside, H.
Flynn, W. H.
Fox, A. J.
Farmer, E.
Fahey, W. H.
Ford, J.
Fredericks, F. C.
Ferguson, Major T. A.
Foote, Lieut. O. C. H.
Foote, Lieut. W. B. H.
Findlay, Lieut. B. B.
Fallon, Lieut. A.
Foster, Lieut. G. B. (M.M.)
French, Capt. C. W. S. (M.C. and Bar)
Fox, Lieut. C. L.
Freeman, Lieut. E. B.
Flannery, Lieut. M. J.
Fraser, Hon. Capt. W. A. (D.S.O.)
FitzHill, Capt. ——

Godfrey, R.
Graham, A. M.
Griffiths, H. E.
Green, H. H.
Greensill, F. W.
Gregory, E.
Grant, W. T.
Galloway, E. G.
Gregory, E. F.
Gill, J. L.
Grey, H.
Geach, C. J.
Grant, W. P.
Gould, S. G.
Grandin, C. P. de C.
Goodworth, F. W.
Green, C.
Griggs, H. W.
Giddens, E. (M.M.)
Gibson, T. H.
Gosper, J.
Gollam, H. A.
Glass, D. K.
Green, T. D.
Gates, D.
Greaves, E. F.
Gray, J. J. (D.C.M.)
Gunn, A. N.
Green, W. A.
Godfrey, R.
Grebber, A. C.
Goodfellow, J. B.

Gilbert, A. H.
Graham, R.
Gibson, J. C.
Giles, M.
Goodwin, R. (M.M. with Bar)
Goode, R. H.
Gordon, F. B.
Goacher, T. J. (M.S.M.)
Garroway, C. E.
Gordon, B. S. (V.C., M.M.)
Gregory, D. A.
Germain, V. (M.M.)
Gibson, G.
Gilbert, R. E.
Greenlees, W. (M.M.)
Gray, A.
Grierson, J.
Grant, B. R.
Green, H. T.
Gundry, G. R.
Grabs, A.
Giblin, J. I.
Greenslade, C.
Gould, E. G.
Gane, J. T.
Goode, R. A. J.
Gallagher, F. A.
Gallagher, F. J.
Gould, J. F.
Grant, R. E.
Gibson, R.
Grierson, E. A.
Goodlands, W.
Grant-Smith, Lieut. J. (M.C.)
Graham, Lieut. C. O.
Graves, Major E. L.
Georgeantis, G.
Greaves, O. V.
Godden, C.
Griffiths, G.
Gill, A.
Gleeson, C.
Geise, F.
Graham, S. G.
Garris, E. T.
Grisinger, J. J.
Grimsey, F. C.
Gosper, E.
Griffin, J. M.
Godfrey, R.
Gardner, S.
Geaghan, M. W.
Gartner, J.
Gleeson, E.
Grambower, G. R.
Graham, C. S. (M.M.)
Garton, H. T.
Gregor, E. G.
Gault, H. J.
Gorman, S. F.
Gardner, E. M.
Guy, G.
Giles, C. G.
Gordon, S.

Glazebrood, I. G.
Guy, E.
Gorven, R.
Griffen, G.
Gray, R. C.
Gibson, J. D.
Gibbons, B. E. B.
Gray, W. L. T.
Colding, L. V.
Greensill, W. F.
Gnatts, J. H.
Graham, W. H.
Gibson, J.
Griffiths, F. M.
Gagen, J. T.
Gleeson, E.
Gardner, W. E.
Garrett, H. H.
Gilmour, H. E.
Gillespie, R.
Green, C. H.
Gray, T.
Given, Lieut. D. W.
Gates, Lieut. D.
Gill, Lieut. G.
Gill, Lieut. J. L.
Gilmour, Lieut. H. E. (M.M.)

Hawthorne, S. S.
Hunter, W. P.
Hine, J. W.
Hendry, J.
Head, J.
Harvey, W.
Henderson, J. S.
Hicks, M. S.
Higgleston, A.
Hossack, W.
Hagger, S. E.
Hays, S. E.
Hunter, C. J.
Harris, T. H.
Holbeck, C. A.
Hall, D.
Harding, G.
Hogan, J.
Harvey, T. J.
Howard, A. V.
Harrison, H. F.
Hourigan, W. J.
Hutchison, J.
Houston, H.
Howie, J. W.
Harding, J. A.
Holton, W. H.
Hopwood, W.
Hall, S.
Hanlon, C. W.
Haimes, F. L.
Holton, G.
Hazell, G. P.
Harward, R. P.
Huddlestone, T. H.

Hamilton, J. S.
Hodgon, W. J.
Harris, C. V.
Haimes, F. W.
Hughes, J. A.
Hill, J. N. (M.M.)
Hendra, W. A.
Haskell, E.
Hodgon, G. L.
Hodgon, C. V. E.
Hancock, J. E.
Hardy, B. U.
Humphries, E. M.
Harvey, S. C.
Hick, J.
Harris, W. J.
Harris, S. D.
Hamilton, E. H.
Hutchison, D.
Hinch, M.
Hawtin, C. E.
Hatchwood, L. J.
Hansen, H. P. J.
Hobbs, W.
Hopkins, H. F.
Hoare, P. M.
Hayes, J.
Harding, P. J.
Higgins, P. W.
Hall, T. B.
Hanley, Lieut. J. J.
Harvey, Lieut. G. W.
Hawtin, Lieut. C. E.
Harley, Lieut. L.
Heron, Lieut.-Col. A. R., C.M.G., (D.S.O.)
Hartigan, M.
Hasthorpe, J. S.
Huxham, A. J.
Hooper, G. W. B.
Hawkins, T. H.
Higgs, R. C.
Holbeck, F. W.
Hatchwell, E. F.
Holden, A. R.
Harding, E.
Hansford, R.
Howes, C. W.
Hill, J. A. A.
Hamilton, M. J.
Houghton, A. V.
Hartley, J.
Hobbs, T. W.
Harvey, W. H.
Hughes, T. W.
Hinchy, D. J.
Hogan, J.
Hill, J.
Hivers, W. H.
Hockings, J.
Haines, C. E.
Hunt, P.
Hermann, C. E.
Hare, H.

Hickey, M. E.
Hancock, H. L.
Hall, W. V.
Hancock, H. L.
Howland, W. J.
Hammersley, W.
Hone, W. A.
Harman, H. J.
Hazzard, W. C.
Hall, V. S. B.
Hawkins, J. H.
Hoelscher, C. G.
Head, J. J.
Horn, T. J.
Hogan, T. J.
Heath, W.
Hobbs, O.
Howell, H. H.
Hughes, H. H. H.
Harris, F. R.
Hall, S.
Hinds, W. M.
Howard, T. M. W.
Hollingsworth, H. O.
Hobbs, T. W.
Hornsby, V.
Heenan, M.
Hardy, W. J.
Hunt, P.
Herbert, J.
Hensly, A. J.
Hynes, M. J.
Howard, W. T.
Hulme, G.
Hagger, H. E.
Hoolihan, J. T.
Hatton, W.
Hartrigsen, C.
Harper, Lieut. H. T.
Harrison, Lieut. P. W.
Howie, Lieut. J. W. (M.C.)
Hamilton, Lieut. H. J.
Hunt, W. J.
Haig, J.
Houghton, F. H.
Hawkins, T. S.
Hampson, T. J.
Hopkins, J. E.
Harris, W. H.
Howard, J. S.
Hunter, H.
Houlihan, C. D.
Harvey, A. R.
Hunter, J. S.
Hawken, F. G.
Hackett, M. P.
Horton, E. J.
Hayes, T. J.
Henry, J. W. E.
Houston, R. C. (M.M.)
Hughes, E. L.
Holloway, H. E.
Haseldon, E. H.
Harper, G. W.

Harvey, R. S.
Huddy, N.
Hoff, A. J.
Hill, B.
Hare, H. J.
Hawkins, A.
Hickey, J.
Hicks, A. W.
Hunter, A.
Harmston, J. S.
Hendry, P. J.
Hay, J.
Hoare, C.
Hughes, T.
Howland, S. J.
Hansen, R. B.
Healy, J. R.
Hancock, D. T.
Hall, W.
Hall, C.
Hall, H. J.
Hall, E.
Hurley, J.
Holman, J. W.
Hemmings, T. J. G.
Harrold, W.
Hambleton, P. A.
Hoskins, R. W.
Hucker, A.
Harvey, J. M.
Heath, G.
Hogan, G.
Hampson, F. L.
Heathcote, W. C.
Henry, T. T.
Hoddinott, F.
Hogan, H.
Henderson, J.
Harris, C. (M.M.)
Hall, E. L.
Hansen, W. P.
Hammond, W. H.
Hetherington, G.
Hilderbrand, L.
Hamlyn, F. A.
Hellings, J. E.
Hepples, J.
Harrison, L.
Hough, J. C. L.
Hodgson, R.
Hayes, I. W.
Hartley, J. B.
Harper, D. H. C.
Hall, S. H.
Harris, E. J.
Harrop, W.
Harris, C. F. W.
Hayes, A. E.
Haffenden, S. J.
Huckle, W.
Hansell, P.
Hine, S. G. R.
Hede, C. T.
Hoopert, C. F.

Hedges, R. E.
Hagen, W. E.
Herd, C. G.
Herbert, E.
Hamilton, J. S.
Hagger, G. H.
Hobson, J. L.
Hansen, H. T.
Harding, F. L.
Hogan, J.
Hopp, H. C. J.
Harth, E. H.
Houlihan, C. J.
Hogarth, A. D.
Hulcombe, J. A.
Hulcombe, G. S.
Hines, W.
Harrison, W. E.
Healy, O.
Harrop, W.
Hanley, G. M. S.
Holland, C. T.
Hopkins, S. J.
Henricks, D. A.
Humber, E. N.
Hansen, H. P.
Heret, H. V.
Hayes, W. J.
Haskins, W.

Ingram, Lieut. H. A. T.
Ingram, T. J.
Innes, A. E.
Ireland, P. A.
Innes, J. T.
Illing, Lieut. F. S.
Ison, R. A. (M.M.)
Ireson, J. T.
Innes, A.
Ingram, F. J.
Inglis, R. A.
Iwers, E. N.
Ironmonger, T.
Ince, H. J.
Isbister, G. (M.M.)
Idol, F. A.

Jones, H. M.
Jones A.
Johnson, C. A.
Jeffrey, A.
Johnson, F. D. (D.C.M.)
Johnson, F. A.
Johnson, W.
Jackson, W.
Jones, V.
Jane, W. H.
Jones, J.
Johnson, W. R.
James, H. W. J.
Jordan, W. W.
Johnson, J. C.

Johnson, W. C.
Jones, W. S. (M.M.)
Jackson, Lieut. L.
Jessen, K. H.
Johnson, J. T.
James, S.
Jones, R. H.
Jary, C. L.
Jones, N.
James-Wallace, Lieut. J. A. (M.M.)
Jones, B. R.
Jones, A. (M.M.)
Jackson, A. P.
Janes, W.
Jansan, I. G.
Jones, P. A.
Jamieson, R. H.
Jamieson, J.
Jackson, T.
Jeffries, W. E.
Jackman, H. L.
Jones, F. L.
Jackson, R. S. C.
James, G.
Jones, R. H.
James, H.
John, W. R.
Johns, A. F.
Johnson, L. H.
Jones, T.
Johnston, C. W. A.
Joanston, R. W.
Jolly, G. E.
Jowett, V. D.
Jakeman, P.
James, J. W.
Johns, J. H.
Johnson, J. F.
Jones, W. A.
Jacklin, W. A.
Jones, R. T.
Joyce, D. J.
Jarvis, J. C.
Johnson, J.
Judd, W. J.
Johnson, A. E.
Juillerat, E. F.
James, H. A.
Jacobsen, F. W.
Jaques, W. L. C.
Jenkins, R.
Jones, Lieut. W. T.

Kelly, E. L.
Kerr, A. H.
Kennedy, J. B.
Kennedy, D.
Kavanagh, M.
Keleher, M. H.
Kennedy, W. F.
Kehl, A. W.
Kehl, A. E.

Kickham, R.
Kelso, J.
Knighton, F.
Kane, H. (M.M.)
Kipping, M.
Kirkman, H. G.
Keith, F. L.
Kerlin, H. A.
Kane, W.
Kavanagh, G.
Knapp, A. A.
Kennedy, W. H.
Kelly, H. J.
King, F.
Kelly, F.
Klaus, C. W.
Klassen, L. J.
Knowles, A.
Keene, F. T.
Kraft, H.
Kew, F. C.
Kerr, W.
Kenyon, A. R.
Kearney, D. L.
Keillor, R. E.
Kerlin, A. S.
Kenman, R. W.
Kielly, W.
Killip, W. F.
Kirby, P.
Kelso, R. J.
Keenan, M.
Kewley, C. J.
Kybert, W. H.
Kirkpatrick, J. K. M.
Kennedy, M.
Kerr, Capt. E.
Kennedy, Lieut. J. J.
Kemp, Lieut. A. R.
Keating, Lieut. W. F.
Knightley, L. H.
Keogh, T.
Kippan, R.
Kelly, J. J.
Kennedy, M.
Kubler, H. H.
Keller, W.
Kelly, F. J.
Kearney, D. G.
Knight, J. W.
Kennedy, W. J.
Keep, J. S.
Kearney, A.
Kostin, W. F.
Kite, W. T.
King, W.
Kelly, J.
Kelly, J. W. J.
Kelly, H. F. P.
Kendall, K. V. E.
Kinsman, E.
Kelly, G.
Knight, R. D.
Kenn, O. R.

Kachel, L. D.
Kirkland, J. A.
Kluck, J. A.
Kennedy, C. L. G.
Kidston, J.

Lyne, J.
Labatt, A.
Larkins, C. J.
Larsgaard, H.
Lawson, J.
Leavey, H.
Lewis, S. W.
Luscombe, P. J.
Love, J.
Lobwein, W.
Lawson, Lieut. J. B. (M.C.)
Lofgren, B.
Lowth, L. G.
Lindsay, W. H.
Likiardopolis, D.
Loseby, F. L.
Love, H. A.
Lang, T.
Lister, T.
Leavey, J. T.
Lynn, J.
Lynn, A. W.
Lowry, F.
Lawler, E.
Leitch, R. Mc.
Leeon, H. W.
Lilly, J. H.
Lamberton, W. J.
Lewis, E. A.
Luke, A.
Lawrence, A. W.
Lawson, R.
Lucas, H.
Lynch, M. J.
Legood, G. W.
Lane, A. J.
Lewis, E. V.
Lipscombe, J. S.
Lowe, A.
Lewis, F. J.
Larkin, Lieut. J.
Lennon, J.
Lewis, J. C. E.
Louden, E.
Louden, D.
Lambert, A. (M.M.)
Lawrence, E. F.
Lingard, F. W. H.
Laxton, T. H.
Lollback, L. E.
Lang, F. W.
Lewis, J.
Lennon, E. G.
Lindsay, W. N.
Lougheed, E. S.
Livingstone, T.
Lougheed, G.

LeGros, J. W. G.
Larsen, G. M.
Lawton, G. H.
Leslie, R.
Long, J.
Lester, B. G.
Leitch, T.
Lyons, J.
Linklater, V.
Loughman, P.
Luton, A. B.
Leathem, G.
Lane, A. B.
Lawrence, A. W.
Lyon, J. L.
Lloyd, A.
Lowther, W. M.
Latcham, A. W.
Leichney, G. Mc.
Large, C. L.
Lee, G. M.
Leeson, J.
Larsen, S.
Lawson, H.
Loxton, W. H.
Ladewig, G. W. L.
Lamb, C. B.
Lowe, J. J.
Lingard, D.
Luscombe, L. G.
Lynch, J. J.
Litzow, R. A.
Livingstone, M.
Livingstone, S.
Lobb, F.
Layfield, F. C.
Lee, J.
Litherland, H. H.
Lochars, O. J.
Lindeman, W. E.
Lees, R. W.
Larsen, H.
Lingard, J. L. E.
Lynch, J. E.
Lacey, R. A. L.
Lambourne, F. H.
Lee, S.
Lucas, R. C.
Lipscombe, W. J.
Lindahl, F. O.
Lorentzen, N. L.
Luxton, J. P.
Luke, A.
Larsen, H. C.
Laing, A.
Langtree, A. T.
Lennon, C. W.
Lait, W. J.
Leslie, A.
Lendrum, T. F.
Larkin, C. J.
Lawrence, E. F.
Lipscombe, J. S.
Large, F. H.

Larsen, H.
Lowther, F. W.
Long, H. H.
Lucas, W. A.
Lathangie, D.
Lee, A. T

Meikle, J.
Myers, F.
Martin, A.
Maby, G. R.
Marshall, F. D.
Martin, W. L.
Mason, L. J.
Mawhinney, W. A.
Meagher, J. V.
Merlehan, C. H.
Moore, J.
Moran, L. V.
Mortimer, H. C.
Mountford, D. A.
Mothersole, A. O.
Miller, J. A.
Martin, A. C.
Mars, J.
Martin, G. R.
Mummery, S. O.
Mazzer, T. H. (M.M.)
Martin, G.
Martin, A.
Martin, E.
Mosely, J.
Marsh, C. E. (M.M.)
Murdoch, G. H.
Mills, F. A.
Mills, A.
Maule, J. R.
Moffatt, J. R.
Moody, J. J.
Magowan, J. J.
Miller, J.
Mills, A. V.
Morrow, C.
Mott, W. G.
Moore, W.
Morrow, W. J.
Macklin, J. R.
Marsh, J.
Middlemiss, R. B.
Meehan, A. S.
Makepeace, E. G.
Maltby, F. (M.M.)
Maltby, T.
Moore, E. J.
Monk, L. S.
Mant, W. H.
Maher, W.
Moss, C.
Markwell, C. S.
Martin, R. B.
Moodie, P.
Morgan, F. R.
Murdoch, J. A.

Mason, B. M.
Morris, A. L.
May, G. A.
Mogan, E. C.
Mann, N. H.
Marks, H. H. S.
Mallam, W. H.
Mathams, G. V.
Mansell, H. J.
Mason, W. G.
Merson, W.
Melling, W.
Murphy, M.
Martin, J.
Mulvenna, J.
Marriott, V. F.
Martin, A. W.
Martin, W.
Martin, W. H.
Martin, W. E.
Moffatt, J.
Mead, D. W.
Matthew, G. H.
Mayes, J. S.
Mitchell, W. G.
Miller, H. C.
Molloy, M.
Morgan, D. R.
Morgan, J.
Murray, W. E.
Mullins, T.
Moxon, P. H.
Munro, W. M.
Moore, W. Mc.
Merlehan, A. E.
Manson, W. J.
Moore, S. N.
Morissey, M.
Montgomery, J. H.
Miles, S. W.
Martin, W. R.
Murphy, J.
Morris, W.
Maroney, J.
Murray, J. C.
Milne, W. J.
Maudsley, A. J.
Moore, W.
Maddock, J. D.
Martindale, P.
Murphy, D. M.
Marsen, A.
Maguire, J. J.
Mavay, H. J.
Mesh, G. H. (M.M.)
Moore, T. S. (M.M.)
Milliard, A. F.
Murphy, A.
Marriott, G. H. A.
Mottershead, T. J.
Mackay, H. B.
Miscampbell, J.
Millward, R. R.
Meredith, F.

Matthews, F. E.
Martyn, F. W.
Mason, C. W. (M.M.)
Muller, O. F. H.
Melville, A. L.
Miller, A. G.
Mason, W. R.
Mahoney, W. R.
Murray, C. H. R.
Millroy, J. C.
Miscamble, E. B.
Morgan, J. E.
Murray, J.
Matthewson, R. F.
Monoghan, R.
Murphy, M. V.
Morris, H.
Murton, A. S.
Maher, G. C.
Mowatt, T. W. W.
Marshall, F.
Morgan, T. P.
Morgan, J.
Moran, M.
Mundle, J. D.
Moodie, T. M.
Mortimer, V. N. H.
Munro, C.
Moore, E.
Maclaren, C. C.
Mills, R.
Moffrey, A. G.
Marshall, A. J.
Moore, S. N.
Mann, F.
Morley, F.
Mackey, D. N. J.
Morgan, J. E.
Mander, J. P.
Matheson, R. F.
Murray, N. S.
Malone, E. V.
Marsh, B. (M.M.)
Miller, Lieut. T. H.
Maher, C. G.
Mitchell, N. S.
Monaghan, R.
Murray, M.
Munsy, J.
Miller, R. J.
Milne, E. A.
Milne, W.
Michael, E. W.
Murray, F. V.
Mawhinney, T.
Mathewson, R.
Moss, Capt. A. H.
Moriarity, Capt. N. S. P.
Moriarty, Lieut. J. J. (M.M.)
Milne, Major J. A. (D.S.O.)
Miller, Capt. F. J. B.
Meyers, Major E. S.
Mills, Major-Chap. A. A. (M.C.)
Murdoch, Lieut. K. A.

Mitchell, Lieut. J. T.
Morgan, G. E.
Miller, P. S.
Marrian, F. W.
Mullan, R. J.
Mann, J. W.
Marsh, E.
Myers, T. N.
Merrin, J.
Mitchell, W. G. A.
Muirhead, L.
Maag, G. H.
Manuel, E.
Mitchell, J. A.
Morgan, F. J.
Massey, H. C.
Mullins, A.
Mahoney, —
Moran, H. M.
Morris, R. C.
Morgan, A.
Mogg, E.
Murdock, A.
Monckton, J.
Maitland, F. W.
Mills, R.
Mahoney, B. A.
Mudge, H. L.
Miles, A. A.
Marshall, A. J.
Murray, N. S. (M.M.)
Murray, R.
Mitchell, R. J.
Moyes, J.
Manning, F.
Martin, G. H.
Maher, P. J.
Moulds, C. H.
Murphy, K. P.
Moloney, T.
Milton, W. W.
Munsie, S. R.
Malyon, C. H.
McCulkin, C. E.
McCullough, J. (M.M.)
McDougall, D. N.
McDougall, J.
McMahon, R. J.
McNab, W. H.
McNeill, R. W.
McCormick, H.
McConaghy, R.
McGregor, P. (M.M. with Bar)
McDonald, W.
McGowan, M.
McLean, Lieut. W. M. (M.C.)
McCartney, T. E.
McAfee, A.
McDougall, D.
McAdam, G. E.
McDonnell, M.
McCulloch, W.
McDade, M.
McFarlane, P.

McDonald, L.
McBean, A. H.
McGregor, G. W.
McGilvery, P. R.
McBean, D.
McConnochie, A.
McDonald, D.
McGrath, J. C.
McAvoy, J. V.
McHugh, F. D.
McWilliam, G.
McLennan, C.
McCartney, V.
McFarlane, J. McD.
McCarthy, B. C.
McFadden, J. B.
McIntosh, D. J.
McLean, R. H.
McQueen, F.
McLaughlin, C. J.
McLellan, J. H. M.
McDonald, J. K.
McLeod, F. A.
McIntosh, A. H.
McDonald, J.
McKinley, C.
McDonald, J. P.
McKelvey, G. R.
McIntosh, P.
McCalla, J. T.
McKee, J. R.
McLennan, R.
McCurley, A. C.
McIntosh, F. S.
McDonald, J. T.
McKenzie, K. C.
McFarlane, J.
McDonald, G. F.
McIvor, E. J.
McIntosh, A.
McClymont, E. V.
McLean, J. B.
McDonald, J.
McMahon, F.
McKenzie, K.
McLaughlin, T. D.
McCullough, J.
McKenzie, J. F.
McCombe, R.
McKie, J. A.
McKenzie, W.
McMahon, M.
McIntosh, S.
McLean, K. E.
McCullock, R. W.
McRobbie, J.
McLardy, R.
McKenzie, R.
McGowan, M.
McAvoy, R.
McLean, C.
McNiff, H. L. J.
McConnell, A. E.
McCleester, A.

McKean, C. W.
McNamara, J. C.
McKennarey, J.
McKean, J. Y.
McHugh, E. W.
McNamara, Hon. Lieut. J.
McPherson, A. J. S.
McKnight, F.
McLennan, G. G.
McLeod, F. A.
McKennon, C. F.
McPherson, P. B.
McCotter, J.
McNeamay, A. L.
McGrath, J. P.
McQueen, H. O.
McDonald, A. J.
McKinley, J.
McGuire, A.
McPaul, G. P.
McKelvery, D. R.
McDonald, T.
McGilvery, E. E.
McClaim, C. C.
McCartney, R. C.
McInnes, P.
McColl, A. R.
McInnes, W.
McKenzie, Lieut. G. C.
McCarthy, Lieut. M. (M.M.)
McIlroy, Capt. R.
MacGibbon, Lieut. F.W. (M.C.)
McCulloch, Lieut. D.

Nelson, A.
Nicoll, R. McQ.
Nicol, J. B.
Nelson, F. J.
Nihill, Lieut. R.
Newman, W. F.
Nunn, T. H.
Nolan, A.
Nugent, M.
Nielsen, F. M.
Neill, A. C.
Nuss, J. J.
Neilsen, N. A. (M.M.)
Neilsen, S. A.
Nicholas, W. H.
North, R. C.
Nagle, J.
Nicholson, W. I.
Nuttall, P. F.
Nolan, M. J.
Norton, W.
Nevin, N.
Normanshaw, F. W.
Newman, D. J. R.
Nash, A. J.
Nilson, N. G.
Nicholson, G.
New, A. G.
Narborough, R. S. C.

Nicol, G. H.
Nevin, G. H.
Norris, C. G.
Newman, J.
Nicholson, J. E.
Nagle, J.
Neumann, E. K.
Nicklin, W. R. M.
Noyes, Lieut. A. F. T.
Nott, G. H. P.
Neal, A. T.
Nix, Lieut. R. B. T.
Nixon, G. H.
Noble, R.

Oliver, H. H.
Otway, T.
Orr, S. G.
Ollson, C. M. S.
Owen, E. K.
Oldmeadow, H. E.
Olson, F.
Offord, T. H.
Otteson, C. W.
Ost, A. M. L.
Owbridge, R. G.
Oliver, J. H.
Oehlmann, W. C.
Olley, R.
Ottosen, C. F.
Olsen, H. E.
Oliver, J. F.
Olsen, W. G.
O'Brien, T.
O'Brien, V. W.
O'Donnell, W.
O'Loan, W.
O'Connell, J.
O'Donnell, L. E.
O'Brien, A. R.
O'Brien, J.
O'Brien, G. E.
O'Connor, J.
O'Connell, A. H.
O'Regan, J.
O'Rourke, J. P.
O'Donohue, E. P.
O'Keefe, J.
O'Neill, O. E.
O'Brien, P. D.
O'Shaughnessy, T.
O'Neill, J.
O'Loughlin, F.
O'Sullivan, F. M.
O'Connor, T. B.
O'Brien, P. F. H.
O'Shaughnessy, S.
O'Niell, L.
O'Reilly, J.
O'Keefe, H.
O'Brien W. E.
O'Farrell, S. M.
O'Connor, J.

O'Neill, J.
O'Sullivan, R.
O'Sullivan, Lieut. T. K.
O'Brien, Capt. R.
O'Bryen, Capt. R. F.
O'Donoghue, W. T. (M.M.)

Paull, W. J.
Parker, W.
Peacock, H.
Pepper, J. W.
Pont, A.
Petersen, W. E.
Pugh, G. H.
Pratt, D.
Pratt, D.
Pettit, C.
Paterson, J. B.
Pearce, A. G.
Prebble, A. W.
Pritchard, J. H.
Porter, C.
Petersen, O. A.
Peters, A. C.
Parker, A. E.
Pacs, W.
Peakes, J. E.
Parminter, J. A.
Pearce, J. E.
Parker, H. G.
Phillips, J.
Pardoe, E. C. R.
Perroux, Lieut. E. F.
Parke, P. F.
Pratt, J.
Patch, V. R. (M.M.)
Purslow, W. A.
Purchase, A.
Pickstone, J.
Phelan, M.
Picot, M. H.
Pemberthy, T. (M.M.)
Penwarn, C.
Plail, A. L.
Platt, W. J.
Platt, G. A.
Pollard, W.
Provians, W. J.
Pickering, W. D.
Petrowski, O. T. J.
Porter, C. C. C.
Philp, A. E. V. (M.M.)
Paxton, H.
Perry, T.
Parsfield, W.
Potter, J.
Perkins, W.
Pearce, S. T.
Palmer, F. J.
Parker, E.
Pakenham, A. E.
Peppercorn, E.
Pishner, H. G.

Palmer, A. H. A.
Petersen, J. E.
Pleavin, R. B.
Pearson, R. J.
Parker, R. H.
Lieut. Pattison, J. G.
Lieut. Parker, W. H.
Peters, J. T. (M.M.)
Parnell, C.
Patch, D. A.
Pascoe, H. L.
Perkins, W. J.
Perkins, R. (M.M.)
Price, A. M.
Pilkington, A.
Pearce, D. A.
Porter, G. C.
Pollard, G. W.
Platt, M.
Pritchard, P.
Perkins, W. E. (M.M)
Pennington, A. H.
Pearman, A.
Pearson, L. E.
Petersen, K. S. B.
Purry, C. B.
Pole, A. J.
Pendery, M.
Peacock, J. C.
Payne, T. B.
Petrie, J. S.
Petersen, C. H.
Pavey, G.
Powell, W. L.
Penrose, H.
Perry, E.
Price, D. T.
Pennicot, R.
Pearson, W. T.
Palmer, A.
Prior, F.
Pokarier, F.
Price, J. J.
Palmer, T. H.
Page, S.
Pool, J. H. F.
Pender, W.
Parker, J. J.
Pennefather, E. K.
Pearson, S.
Paterson, T. I.
Parker, W. L.
Pacey, R.
Price, C H.
Paterson, D.
Percy, D.
Parker, A. W.
Pursehouse, E. T.
Pierce, A. R.
Parsloe, H. C.
Picking, C. R.
Powell, V. G.
Petersen, A. H.
Parkes, J. G.

Prestidge, H.
Price, Lieut. E. D. (M.C.)
Pickering, Capt. R. F.

Quigley, A.
Quinlivan, G.
Quinn, M. J.
Quinn, W. T.
Quinn, T. F.

Robinson, Lieut. S. L. (M.C.)
Ross, W.
Redbond, P.
Rahal, T. P.
Reah, O.
Reid, A. J.
Reid, R. W.
Roberts, G. E.
Robinson, W. H.
Roy, S.
Roos, O. E.
Rumsey, J.
Robbie, G.
Roberts, S. A.
Rooney, W.
Rodda, V. H.
Reid, W. F.
Reid, R.
Richardson, A.
Regan, T.
Ringer, W. H.
Round, G.
Rogers, Lieut. L. H.
Reeves, J. A.
Reilly, J. (D.C.M.)
Rough, W. H. (M.M.)
Ralph, W.
Rodger, A. G.
Robertson, A. B.
Robson, J. H.
Rowbottom, G. H.
Rowe, W.
Royan, A. J.
Reid, J. E. C. H.
Roots, H. J.
Robinson, J. R.
Robinson, H.
Roberts, J. S.
Riddle, A. G.
Ralph, C. (M.M.)
Roberts, V. H.
Ross, H. A.
Ramsay, E. E.
Russell, J.
Reid, J. W.
Riordan, W.
Rickard, F. C.
Ramm, P. A.
Rendle, N. (M.M.)
Rickwood, B. W. (D.C.M.)
Richardson, C. L.
Richardson, J.

Rigg, Lieut. P. R.
Rolfe, E. G.
Roberts, Lieut. R. H. O.
Roberts, M.
Round, F. W.
Rix, M. A.
Russell, W. H.
Robertson, T. H.
Rowton, R.
Ransom, A. R.
Ranson, G. V.
Robertson, A. H.
Robinson, Lieut. G. S. H.
Ross, P. W.
Russell, C. (M.M.)
Reay, L. A.
Ross, H. H. (M.M.)
Richardson, Lieut. T. C.
Richardson, Lieut. G.
Redmond, Capt. J.
Robertson, Lieut. J. H.
Robinson, M. O.
Roberts, ——
Rowlands, S. L.
Randell, J.
Robertson, J. H.
Reynolds, A. J.
Rudd, R. J. P.
Rake, J. V.
Radcliffe, T.
Ries, W. M.
Rivett, R. R.
Rundle, E. R.
Redit, G.
Robbins, A. F.
Ross, D.
Rainey, J. H.
Riding, C. J.
Reynolds, W. M.
Renouf, E. C.
Rowatt, R. J.
Rose, H. E.
Redshaw, G.
Rogers, A. A.
Reid, W. E.
Reid, W.
Ramsay, J.
Robinson, F.
Roughead, E.
Ryan, J.
Renton, H.
Rapp, G. K.
Rose, A.
Richardson, A. S.
Rankan, F. G.
Ray, J. P.
Rutherford, C.
Ryan, A. J.
Rattle, W.
Robertson, G. W.
Rainey, J. H.
Rapkins, H. T.
Rutherford, R. E.
Reynolds, A.

Reid, S.
Robinson, W. G.
Rose, F.
Ramsay, J. A.
Rolfe, W. R.
Reynolds, H. S.
Rump, A. W.
Reid, W. E.
Read, G. J. H.
Ragh, A. W.
Roginson, C.
Rake, G. A.
Rowbottom, A. F.
Roberts, A. H.
Router, C. H.
Richards, L.
Rasmussen, F.
Richards, B.
Randall, W. W.
Reading, J. C.
Roy, P.
Rolfe, G.
Russell, J.
Ross, D. J.
Rowland, W. H.
Rogers, A. V.
Retchless, R. D.
Robinson, S.
Ryle, A. W.
Rogers, A. A.
Riding, W. J.

Strong, H. J.
Small, W.
Sadleir, E. D.
Scheiller, P. C.
Seddon, H. H.
Seymour, W.
Shea, T. (M.M.)
Shields, M.
Shortridge, B. C.
Simpkins, J.
Simpson, J.
Sinclair, H. E.
Smith, D. R.
Snelson, W.
Steine, W. E.
Stevenson, J.
Stevenson, J.
Stolz, G. H.
Stockham, H.
Shannon, F. O.
Sabadine, E. E.
Skinner, G. R.
Street, C. H.
Street, J. F.
Self, M.
Scanlon, J.
Skelton, G. W.
Spence, W.
Spence, S. N.
Stone, A. H.
Stevens, A. L. (M.M.)

Sexton, J.
Stanford, R.
Smith, F. W.
Sim, L. W.
Skugar, G. M. (M.M.)
Short, A.
Solomons, D. S.
Samuels, T.
Schroder, N. R.
Smith, R. L.
Stirratt, R.
Swindall, J.
Stewart, R. H.
Stephenson, E. H.
Stephenson, J. T.
Smith, G. M.
See, C.
Secomb, Lieut. W. C.
Suares, W. J.
Smith, G. A.
Stuhmcke, H.
Sharman, H. J.
Snell, W.
Shales, J. F. (M.M.)
Saunders, R. V.
Simpson, E. R.
Swan, D. T.
Smith, A. J.
Simpson, J. C.
Snow, S. R. (M.M.)
Skinner, J.
Sorenson, J. A.
Smith, W.
Stoyle, J. B.
Sawtell, R.
Schumacher, W. C.
Shearer, J.
Sheather, A. H.
Shields, W. D.
Sims, J. W.
Smith, H. W.
Smith, R. B.
Solomon, J. C.
Sutherland, D.
Swanstrom, A. O.
Staines, C. J.
Scriven, J.
Sonneman, F. H.
Sheehan, W.
Shepherd, W. O.
Schmidt, H. W.
Shirley, A.
Seaforth, P. G.
Sheehan, W. J.
Sharkey, S. H.
Smith, T. C.
Slattery, T. J.
Stuart, A. R.
Shearman, W. C.
Stehn, C. J. (M.M.)
Speedy, J. J.
Sherwin, G. E.
Sherwin, T. H.
Schumacher, E. T. (M.M.)

Sturgess, H. G.
Stanton, W. N.
Smith, H. H.
Schemallech, L.
Sowdy, F. W.
Streeter, T. H.
Skiffington, T. P.
Storey, F.
Smith, H.
Smith, R. J.
Stutz, R. J. (M.M.)
Schmidt, H. F.
Smith, J.
Schipke, D. C. A.
Sawyer, A. W.
Stolzenhern, P.
Shore, C. N.
Stevens, S. H.
Sims, A. E.
Stevenson, J. A.
Stevenson, J.
Shambrook, E. C.
Sharp, W. G.
Spence, W. R.
Smith, R. A.
Smith, A. B.
Sackett, H. A.
Savage, A. H.
Swinghammer, C.
Stapleton, G. J.
Sigley, J.
Slater, T. H.
Skene, C. S.
Stevenson, D.
Sullivan, J. R.
Smallwood, V. E. P.
Scarborough, R.
Smith, L.
Stack, E. J.
Switzer, W. J.
Sheppard, W. H.
Smart, A. G. (M.M.)
Sikkema, H. C.
Sutton, R.
Strike, E.
Sharp, A. McG.
Scholz, R.
Sherwood, J. H.
Stover, W. J. T. G.
Smith, R.
Shanahan, J.
Smith, P.
Shearing, E. J.
Spackman, H. G.
Skelton, W.
Steers, H. R.
Smith, A.
Stuart, A. R.
Stevens, C.
Swanson, R. M.
Sparks, F. J.
Sibbles, D. C. A. (M.M.)
Shearman, E.
Skinner, W.

Smith, A. H.
Schooler, J.
Sanderson, F. J.
Smith, J.
Smith, R. W. H.
Stone, H. J.
Silvester, A. G.
Sim, J. L.
Sigg, A.
Stafford, W.
Slatter, F. L.
Studt, C. F.
Sait, W.
Swinghammer, V. G.
Savage, P. D.
Smith, E.
Scholes, R. N. M.
Skandgnist, F. J.
Steele, J.
Stephens, E. J.
Stephens, W.
Savage, D.
Stringer, M. C.
Starkey, W. W.
Silcock, S. L.
Skinner, J.
Sweeney, D.
Smith, J. J.
Seabrooke, P.
Sills, R. W.
Soorley, W. R.
Scanlon, D.
Stitchnoth, F.
Sandiland, A.
Staunton, N. B.
Sketchley, W. P.
Smith, E.
Stevens, E. E.
Smith, N. E.
Siemon, S. S.
Smallhorn, R. S.
See, S.
Scott, W. A.
Smith, J. A.
Sambourne, F.
Simpson, A. E.
Stern, W.
Stuckey, H. J.
Spreadborough, J. R.
Stubbs, L. C.
Stevens, R. E.
Skelton, W. G.
Sides, J. A. L.
Seeney, A.
Stirling, W.
Saunders, L.
Smith, T.
Smith, J.
Steene, W. E.
Samson, G. F.
Selby, J. W.
Stitt, H. A.
Smith, W. M.
Sinclair, J. V.

Shannon, F. O.
Staines, C. J.
Sherrin, G. S.
Smith, C. L. (M.M.)
Stephenson, C. G.
Standen, J. E.
Smyth, A. E.
Sadd, A.
Schmidt, B.
Skyrme, F. L.
Smith, H. J.
Smith, G. E.
Scanlon, T.
South, R. J.
Spackman, H. G.
Saunders, R.
Seeney, A.
Shaum, C. J. E.
Smith, J. H.
Stuart, W. J.
Shapcott, H. S.
Stenzel, A.
Skerman, W.
Sykes, F. L.
Somerville, J.
Spreen, R.
Shannon, W. P.
Storen, J.
Sanders, E. H.
Smith, J.
Summers, A. E.
Stickley, S. K.
Smith, Lieut. W. (M.M.)
Schroder, Lieut. N. R.
Smith, Lieut. H.
Skewes, Lieut. A. W.
Savage, Lieut. A. H.
Stratford, Lieut. F. W.
Stanley, Lieut. A.
Smith, Lieut. L. M.
Sheridan, Major E. T.
Swanson, Capt. P. M.
St. John, Capt. A. P. (M.C.)

Turnbull, W. A.
Toomey, E. F.
Tree, W. W.
Trotman, E. J.
Turner, H.
Turner, P.
Thomas, F.
Thygesen, C. W.
Turner, G. H.
Tripcony, T. M.
Thomas, N. J.
Tobiason, E. W.
Thompson, A. H.
Tredenick, Lieut. R.
Thomas, A.
Tape, P. J.
Topfer, W. R.
Thompson, A.

Thornberry, H. A.
Turnbull, W.
Taylor, J. L.
Trimble, G. R.
Tutt, C. W. E.
Tyrell, E. J.
Thompson, J. W.
Tyler, E. D.
Tigell, L. D.
Taylor, A.
Terry, H.
Traill, G.
Taylor, W. J.
Taylor, J. A.
Taylor, B.
Toohey, T.
Thornton, R. B.
Tobin, E. A.
Trenkner, F.
Thorpe, E. A. A.
Thompson, G. E.
Tunley, L. W.
Teague, J. W.
Tritton, G.
Tytherleigh, S.
Thies, G.
Thompson, J. E.
Taylor, A.
Tuckey, C. W.
Thompson, J. S.
Thorpe, J.
Thatches, G.
Thompson, C.
Thompson, A. M.
Turner, V. J.
Thomas, F. A.
Thompson, F.
Tooth, S. W.
Turnstall, V.
Thompson, F. F.
Thomasson, R. J.
Thompson, J.
Thacker, E.
Train, S.
Thompson, N.
Toohey, E.
Tranter, F. D.
Thompson, J. E.
Trenery, T. J.
Thomas, Capt. G.
Taylor, Lieut. T. G.
Tardent, Lieut. J. L.
Trudgian, Lieut. C. S. (M.C.)
Tillidge, Lieut. C.
Todd, Lieut. E. C.
Tanner, Lieut. A. B.
Thompson, A. J.
Turner, R.
Treherne, A. T.
Thompson, E.
Thain, C.
Tunny, J.
Tanzer, W. G.
Tunny, F. P.

Twose, A. W.
Tyson, W.
Tesch, H. J.
Toby, R. T. F.
Thornburn, A. McT.
Thomas, E. W.
Thompson, J. J.
Thorn, M. W.
Toomey, A.
Thow, C. E.
Thomas, M.
Tallis, P. N.
Tomlinson, D. M.
Taylor, W. E.
Tynan, M. J.
Tratt, G.

Uscinski, V.
Uhlmann, J. R.
Urquhart, M. T.
Ubank, S. J.
Ulrick, J. O.
Unwin, F. E. J.
Unicomb, A.
Capt. Uren, W.

Venton, G. J.
Voice, J.
Vary, K. W. J.
Vagne, G. S.
Vann, G. A.
Vesperman, L. H.
Vautin, F. T.
Verrall, N.
Vassallo, E.
Vaughan, A. J.
Vickery, W. T.
Vinson, D. J.
Vaughan, D. K.

Willis, C. W.
Willey, W. H.
Watters, J. A.
Walker, J. M.
Walmsley, P. O.
Walsh, E. T.
Waters, M. L.
Watkins, W. C.
Watts, A. J.
Wellspring, T. C.
White, E. G. D.
Wickham, L. H.
Wiseman, J.
Williams, A. E.
Williams, E. J.
Williams, G. A.
Williams, F. E.
Williams, W. H.

Wilson, E. A.
Wood, A. D.
Woods, J.
Walker, H.
Wettenhall, L. C.
Williamson, H. E.
Williamson, P.
Warry, V. R.
Woods, C. S.
Winterbottom, D.
Webb, A.
Waters, H.
Whitting, W. P.
Wakely, F.
Woods, F. J.
Wood, E. W.
Wardill, T.
Wyton, A. F.
Wilson, C.
Wicks, A. J.
Wilson, J.
Woodford, J. E.
Weir, D. T.
Willcox, P. (M.M.)
Weinert, F.
Watego, M.
Webb, J. E.
Wilkins, H. T.
Watson, A. A. C.
Ward, F.
Woodhouse, W. W.
Wrather, L.
Wilson, R. A.
Wright, J.
Wilkinson, J.
Waind, A.
Williams, W.
Wolfe, W. J.
Wynn, S.
Weatherhead, F.
Wise, G.
Williamson, G.
Whitecross, W. M. L.
Wilson, F. G.
Watson, J. T.
Wilcher, T. J.
Whitecross, A. S.
Wheeler, D. B.
Wellings, Lieut. L.
Wood, Lieut. R. R.
Wood, Lieut. M. C.
Williams, Lieut. E. A.
Wood, Lieut. J. F.
Wright, Lieut. T.
Watson, T.
Waldron, W. F.
Weatherstone, G.
Walsh, T. J.
Weeks, S. W. (D.C.M.)
Wenman, T. F.
Willcox, M.

Williams, G.
Wood, G.
Whannell, J. (M.M.)
Wornes, R. A.
Wayman, C. H.
Wickman, H.
Wardrop, E. C.
Waddell, R. L.
Woodward, H.
Waldron, J.
White, H. S.
Willis, C. J.
Wilesmith, A. W.
Warren, E.
Webb, R.
Watt, T.
Wise, T. A.
Ward, W. A.
Welch, C. F.
Wiseman, R. C.
Williams, G. E.
Watson, J.
Williams, L. E.
Wallace, A. B.
Wilkinson, W.
Watts, A. T.
Wright, F.
Williams, G.
Walsh, V. H.
Wilkie, R. (M.M.)
West, A. N.
Williams, D. M.
Watt, H.
White, W.
Whitney, C. R.
Wright, J. E.
Wilson, G. M.
Wallace, H. H. A.
Watts, N. A. H.
Wilkie, W. J. (M.M.)
Watson, A. W. F.
Woodcock, E.
Walters, W.
Wratten, W. J.
White, C. E.
Warren, T.
Ward, D. W.
Woodruffe, J. S.
Ward, J. J.
Williams, B. C.
Waters, G.
Watson, H. A.
Wallace, D. T.
Wilkie, O. R.
Wade, E.
Wallace, A. E.
Walker, J. W. (D.C.M.)
Wiles, Lieut. H. J. (D.S.O.)
Woodfort, Lieut. J. E.
Witham, Hon. Lieut. H. M.
Wilson, Lieut. G. C. C.

Walker, Lieut. J. R. H.
Whiteside, Lieut. P. G.
White, H.
Lieut. Watts, H. T.
Wood, J. B.
Wyatt, V. E.
Wilson, M. E.
Wriggles, H. F.
Wright, W. M.
Wright, F. G.
Webb, J. W.
Weston, R.
Windsor, G. R.
Waldron, J.
Walsh, W. N.
Williams, O. O.
Wilford, F.
Wood, C. J.
Webster, J. T.
Wright, R.
Williams, N.
Walsh, W. D.
Williams, G. H.
Walker, A. R.
Wilson, T. N.
Winthrop, N. E.
White, J. H.
Ward, W. F.
Walsh, R. J.
Walsh, C. J.
Welsh, E. W.
Whitely, P.
Weave, F.
Wakeman, H. C.
White, E. G. D.
Wood, P. A.
Williams, A. G.
Wilkins, I.
Wilton, H.
Woodhead, C. F.
Walker, D. W.
Watt, N. A.
White, L. E. G.
Walsh, D. I.
Wood, R. R.
Williams, D.
Wardlaw, J.
Wilson, R. E.
Wolfe, E. J.
Watts, L. A.
Wingett, A. J.
Weeks, J.
Witherwick, R.
White, A. C.
Winks, C. N. J.
Ward, R. A.
White, H. C.
Weldon, W. H.
Wasley, J. H.
Watts, A.
Wilson, A.

Watts, H. C.
Winston, A.
Walsh, R. J.
Wallace, A. E. D.
Walsh, J. M.
Weathered, J. F.
Winzar, H. S.
West, A. H.
White, K.
Wardrop, R. A. S.
Wilson, W. H.
Williamson, G. H.
Wills, J. H.
Wait, A. E.
Walsh, R.
Wayman, W.
Wyatt, H. G.
Walker, B. R.
Wright, C. A.
Wilson, A. G.
Wells, R.
Wicklegren, W.
West, R.
Williams, H.
Wakefield, C. F. D.
Willis, E. G.
Walters, W.
Watts, L. A.
Walsh, L. M.
Wells, H.
Wilson, S. L.
Wynd, H.
White, A. R. B. H.
Wilkie, G. S.
Waugh, J. C.
Walters, A. A.
West, C. H.

Yule, A. C. D.
Yates, J. F.
Yenton, G. J.
Young, T.
Yates, W. J.
York, E. A.
Young, S. J.
Yates, F. W.
Young, C. T.
Yensch, H. G.
Young, T.
Young, F. G.
Young, D.
Young, J. A.
Yell, B. A.
Yarker, J.
Young, V. G.
Young, W. D.

Zingleman, F.
Zimmerle, H.
Zahner, J. G.

List of Honours and Awards

Victoria Cross.
L./Cpl. Gordon, B. S.

Companion St. Michael and St. George.
Lt.-Col. Heron, A. R. (D.S.O.)

Distinguished Service Order.
Lt.-Col. Heron, A. R.
Lieut. Fraser, W. A.
Lieut. Wiles, H. J.

Bar to Military Cross.
Lieut. Butler, C. H.
Capt. French, C. W. S.

Military Cross.
Chap.-Major Mills, A. A.
Lieut. McLean, W. M.
Lieut. Price, E. D.
Lieut. Boyce, L. A. G.
Lieut. Howie, J. W.
Lieut. Butler, C. H.
Lieut. Burtenshaw, F. J.
Lieut. Robinson, S. L.
Capt. French, C. W. S.
Lieut. Grant-Smith, J.
Lieut. Lawson, J. B.
Lieut. Brown, D.
Capt. Calow, P. F.
Lieut. MacGibbon, F. W.

Distinguished Conduct Medal.
Sgt. Weeks, W. S.
Sgt. Edwards, A.
L./Cpl. Dean, J.
Pte. Breen, A. J.
Cpl. Rickwood, B. W.
L./Cpl. Reilly, J.
Pte. Gray, J. J.
L./Cpl. Dun, J. C.
Pte. Dixon, E. (M.M.)
Cpl. Johnson, F. D.
Pte. (now L./Cpl.) Walker, J.
Sgt. Carlson, C.

Meritorious Service Medal.
Sgt. Ferguson, J. M.
Sgt. Goacher, T. J.
Sgt. Phillips, J.

Bar to Military Medal.
Pte. McGregor, P.
C.S.M. Goodwin, R.

Military Medal.
Sgt. (now Lieut.) Moriarty, J. J.
Sgt. (now Lieut.) Smith, W.
Sgt. Nielsen, N. A.
Pte. Rendle, N.
Pte. McCullough, J.
Pte. Shea, T.
Pte. Russel, C.
Pte. Dunsford, A. G.
Sgt. Hill, J. N.
Cpl. Ison, R.
Pte. McGregor, P.
Pte. Shales, J. F. G.
Pte. Adam, R. J.
Pte. Wilkie, W. J.
Sgt. (now Lt.) James-Wallace, J. A.
Pte. Carter, T.
Sgt. Greenlees, W.
Pte. Durrington, A. A.
Cpl. Mesh, G. H.
Sgt. Maltby, F.
Sgt. Dodd, H. H.
L./Cpl. Lambert, A.
L./Cpl. Ashton, E. D.
Driver Kane, H.
L./Cpl. Perkins, R.
Pte. Stutz, R. J.
Pte. Bryant, R. J.
Pte. Stehn, C. J.
Pte. Marsh, C. E.
Pte. Fitzgerald, T.
Pte. Ashwood, E.
Cpl. Ralph, C.
Pte. Dixon, E. (D.C.M.)
Sgt. Cuddy, L. C.
Pte. Whannel, J.
Pte. Penberthy, T.
Pte. Cook, E. W.
Pte. Moore, T. S.
Cpl. Germain, V.
Pte. O'Donoghue, W. T.
Pte. Stevens, A. R.
Pte. Isbister, G.
Pte. Wilkie, R.
Pte. Costello, B. W.
Pte. Patch, V. R.
Pte. Dick, J. R.
Pte. Giddens, E.
Pte. Mason, C. W.
Pte. Forsyth, W. J.
Pte. Cox, W. L.
L./Cpl. Gordon, B. S. (V.C.)
C.S.M. (now Lt.) Burnett, G. O.
Pte. Philp, A. E. V.
Pte. Skugar, G. M.
L./Cpl. Briskey, W. C.
Sgt. Armstrong, J. T.
Pte. Jones, A.
C.S.M. Goodwin, R.
Pte. Dwyer, J. J.
Cpl. Schumacher, E. T.
Pte. Cleland, G. R.
Pte. Houston, R. C.
L./Cpl. Brown, W. C.
Sgt. Jones, W. S.
Driver Boyle, H. P.
Pte. Fuller, T. G.
Pte. Ansell, C. J.
L./Sgt. Rough, W. H.
Cpl. Mazzer, T. H.
Pte. Frederickson, R. M.
L./Cpl. Woolccck, P. J.
Pte. Ellis, C. B.
Cpl. Harris, C.
Sgt. Sibbles, F.
Sgt. Culluc, G. L.
Pte. Ross, H. H.
Pte. Perkins, W. E.
L./Sgt. Follington, T. D.
Cpl. Snow, S. R.
Pte. Graham, C. S.
Pte. Smart, A. G.

Belgian Croix de Guerre.
Capt. Pickering, R. F.
Sgt. Colville, F. A.
Pte. Graham, A. M.

Mentioned in Despatches.
Pte. Costello, B. W. (M.M.)
Lt.-Col. Heron, A. R. (C.M.C., D.S.O.; third occasion)
Major Ferguson, T. A.
Lieut. Brewer, R.
Lieut. Murdoch, K. A.
Lieut. Price, E. D. (M.C.)
C.S.M. Goodwin, R. (M.M.)
Pte. Howell, W.
Lieut. Fraser, W. A. (D.S.O.)
Lt. MacGibbon, F. W. (M.C.)
Capt. Swanson, P. M.
Lieut. Wiles, H. K. (D.S.O.)
Sgt. Bletcher, V.

Brevet Promotion of Major.
Lt.-Col. Heron, A. R. (C.M G.) (D.S.O).
Major T. A. Ferguson.

Honor Roll of the 41st Battalion, A.I.F.

Ahbol, L. E.
Asche, Lieut. F. H.
Aris, B.
Abbott, F. W.
Adams, J.
Allen, T.
Andrews, W. W.
Atkinson, F. D.
Anderson, H. H.
Allan, J.
Archbold, W. J.
Anderson, C. A. (M.C.)
Anderson, A. A.
Armstrong, G.
Ault, A. H.
Adams, J.
Alexander, C. D.

Blayney, W.
Burns, F.
Brown, F.
Beitz, W. F.
Barryman, A. E.
Bartlett, G. F.
Byrnes, W. C.
Bentham, W.
Barker, S. T.
Buzza, D. W.
Burke, J.
Blackman, A. G.
Bailey, A. G.
Brandt, A.
Boutle, L. R.
Bell, W. J.
Brown, G.
Browning, H.
Bente, H. C.
Burtenshaw, Lieut. F. J. (M.C.)
Byrnes, A. H.
Brown, A.
Bremner, A. G.
Bryson, A.
Brooks, P.
Bryce, J. J.
Brown, Lieut. D.
Brooks, O. V.
Brewer, Lieut. R.
Bennett, A.
Blinman, H.
Bramley, A. A.
Beresford, C.
Bauer, W. A.
Branson, C. H.
Bennett, A.
Beggs, L. C.
Bashforth, G. T.
Bardwell, H. W.
Barrie, J.
Brooks, G. W.

Claydon, A. W.
Cupples, B. A.
Cuddy, E. H. G.
Cotterell, H. J.
Crowe, J. J.
Claydon, W.
Cummins, W. D.
Cook, A.
Campbell, L. H.
Cantwell, L. E.
Coe, L.
Campbell, L. J.
Coppins, W.
Carr, A. C.
Cummins, T. P.
Conn, R. C.
Charles, J. H.
Carrie, J. E.
Clarke, N. W.
Claridge, R. O. J.
Chandler, E. J.
Campbell, J.
Cottell, H. V.
Clews, J. A. B.
Croft, E.
Cooke, S. R.
Cowan, T. J.
Carstens, C. N.
Connor, C. E.
Clark, F. L. R.

Dodds, H. H.
Dickie, Lieut. A.
Davis, W. E.
Duffy, E. C.
Dean, J. A.
Downton, C.
Daniel, A. F.
Donaldson, A.
Dixon, V.
Duffy, R. W.
Dykes, G. P.
Dale, H. H.
Drylie, R.
Davidson, G.
Dyson, S.
Duffy, A.
Draddy, J. T. P.
Dumbrell, W. W.
Donaldson, A. C.
Dougherty, W.
Dun, J. C.
Dodds, Lieut. G. S.
Dunsford, A. G.
Deeves, C. H.
Durrington, A. A.

Dale, E. T.
Davis, C. A.
Dickson, J. E.
Delacour, P. J.
De Reeve, E. J.

Epps, Lieut. J. H.
Early, W. G.
Elms, B. G.
Eccles, A. E.
Ellem, B. A.
Ellem, W. A.

Fogg, G. H.
Freeman, A.
Funnell, G.
Freemantle, A.
Freshwater, A. J.
Fitzgerald, J.
Farrelly, S. P.
Fitzmaurice, L. G.
Forsyth, N. A.
Fitzgerald, T.
Ferrari, J.
Ford, W.
Fibbins, A.

Gallagher, F. J.
Gray, A.
Glass, D.
Geach, C. J.
Greenhill, W. F.
Gallagher, F. J.
Griffen, J. M.
Gardner, S.
Greber, A. C.
Grisinger, J. J.
Grandin, G. P.
Grant, W. P.
Gregory, E. F.

Hare, H.
Hazzard, W. C.
Hill, J.
Hamilton, E. H.
Harrison, H. J.
Howell, W.
Harvey, T. J.
Hall, D.
Hooper, C. W. B.
Haines, C. E.
Harvey, G. W.
Haggar, S. E.
Hinch, M.
Hopp, H.
Hogan, J.
Harvey, W.
Higgs, R. C.
Hailes, F. L.
Harley, G.
Harth, C. H.
Hall, V. R.
Holton, G.
Hoskins, R. W.
Hemmings, T. J. G.
Hughes, H. H.
Harris, C. V.
Hendry, J.
Harrison, L.
Henderson, J.
Houghton, A. V.
Hone, W. A.
Henry, J. W. E.
Herbert, J.
Harper, D. H. C.
Hagger, H. E.
Hodgon, W. J.
Hamilton, M. J.
Harman, H. J.

Innes, A. E.

Jones, H. M.
Jones, B. R.
Jones, W. A.
Johnson, J. C.
James, G.

Kippen, R.
Kemp, Lieut. A. R.
Klassen, J. L.
Keilor, R. E.
Kehl, A. E.
Kerr, Capt. E.
Kelso, J.
Kelly, F.
Kostin, W. F.
Keen, F. T.
Keogh, T.
Kendall, K. V. E.
Kelso, R. J.

Laxton, T. H.
Larkin, Lieut. J.
Langtree, A. T.
Lendrum, T. F.
Lang, A. E.
Loudon, E.
Lawler, E.
Legood, G. W.
Lingard, F. H.

Lollback, L. E.
Love, H. A.
Lillingstone, T.
Lindsay, W. N.
Lucas, R. C.
Lawson, J.
Lowth, L. G.
Lougheed, E. S.
Lindeman, W. E.
Lawson, Lieut. J. B. (M.C.)
Lougheed, G.
Loseby, F. L.
Lowther, W. M.
Lowther, F. W.
Lilly, J. H.
Lewis, J.

Martin, W. E.
Merlehan, C. H.
Mills, A.
Moran, L. V.
Moore, W.
Merlehan, A. E.
Mallam, H. W.
Moran, M.
Marsen, A.
Maltby, T.
Makepeace, E. G.
Matthews, G. H.
Mountford, D. A.
Moore, S. M.
Murphy, J. C.
Marshall, A. J.
Markwell, C. S.
Mitchell, Lieut. J. T.
Marks, H. H. S.
Mesh, G. H.
Morrow, C.
Moody, T. M.
Myers, T. N.
Meagher, J. V.
Maddock, J. D.
Mowatt, T. W. W.
Morgan, J.
Mansell, J. H.
Murray, J. C.
Mavey, H. J.
Maag, G. H.
Mead, V. D.
Munro, C.
McLennon, G. C.
McNab, W. H.
McCafferty, E. S.
McFarlane, L. McD.
McIntosh, D. J.
McWilliam, G.
McDonald, D. G.
McKinley, C.
MacGowan, J.
McDade, M.
McIntosh, S. K.
McMahon, R. J.
McBean, N. A.

Nagle, J.
Nicol, J. B.
Nuss, J. J.
Neil, A. C.
Norton, W.
Nelson, F. J.

O'Neill, J.
O'Regan, P.
Ost, A. M. L.
O'Connor, J.
O'Sullivan, Lieut. T. R.
O'Donnell, W.

Paul, W. J.
Palmer, A. H. A.
Pishner, H. G.
Pakenham, A. E.
Pollard, W.
Pugh, G.
Platt, C. A.
Platt, W. J.
Petersen, W. E.
Pritchard, H. J.
Parker, W.
Parke, P. F. H.
Pascoe, H. L.
Plail, A.
Peacock, H.
Pratt, D.
Pont, A.
Porter, C.
Pierce, A. R.
Petrie, J. S.
Price, C. H.
Pennington, A. H.
Parker, H. G.
Pickering, W. D.
Pearson, L. E.
Pearman, A.
Philp, A. E. V.

Quinn, M. J.

Rapp, G. K.
Robinson, H. W.
Roberts, N.
Rowbottom, C. H.

Ross, P. W.
Reid, R. W.
Robertson, D. A. H.
Robinson, Lieut. G. S. H.
Ries, W. M.
Rigg, Lieut. R. P.
Robertson, G.
Roberts, Lieut. R. H. O.
Rickwood, B. W.
Reay, L. E.
Rowbottom, A. F.
Round, W. F.
Robertson, T. H.
Redmund, Capt. J.

Sterling, W.
Stewart, W. J.
Shields, W. D.
Stevenson, J.
Snell, W.
Sabadine, E. E.
Slattery, T. J.
Strong, H. S.
Storey, F.
Skewes, Lieut. A. W.
Swindall, J. W.
Shortridge, B. C.
Shannon, F.
Spence, S. N.
Stevenson, L.
Siemon, S. S.
Smith, A. H.
Sutton, R.
Stanford, R.
Sheather, A. H.
Smith, G. E.
Stuckey, H. J.
Slater, T. H.
Sherwin, G. E.
Spence, W.
Smith, H. J.
Stevenson, J.
Stewart, R. H.
Skinner, G. R.

Thompson, A. J.
Taylor, Lieut. T. G.
Thygesen, P. A.
Taylor, J. A.
Thompson, J. W.
Tyson, W.
Tape, J. P.
Thacker, E.
Teague, J. W.
Turner, G. H.
Thompson, J. J.
Tutt, C. W. E.
Trotman, E. J.
Tuckey, C. W. D.
Thomas, F. F.

Ubank, S. J.
Uren, Capt. W.

Venton, G. J.

Wriggles, H. F.
Wilsher, F. J.
Watson, T. E.
Whitting, W. P.
Weatherstone, J.
Wellings, Lieut. L.
Wise, F. S.
Walsh, V. H.
Wilson, Lieut. G. C. C.
Whyte, H. S.
Wiseman, R. F.
Wilkins, H. L.
Ward, W. A.
Watters, J. A.
Warren, E.
Watson, A. C. A.
Wilson, R. A.
Williams, G.
Wettenhall, L. C.
William, E. J.
Windsor, G. R.
Wright, W.
West, A. N.
Wilson, F. G.
Watt, N. A.
Waldron, F. W.
Watson, H. A.
Warren, T.
Welch, C. F.
Woodford, Lieut. J. E.
Williams, F. J.
Walters, W.
Wilkinson, W.
Weeks, W. S.
Webb, A.
Wood, A. D.
Wrather, L.
Williams, G. E.
Wilson, R. E.
Wallace, D. T.
Woodward, H.
Winks, C. J.
Waters, M. L.
Wilson, E. H.
Wickham, L. H.
Williams, L. E.
Wakefield, C. F. D.

Yates, W. J.
Yates, J.
Young, D.

Zingleman, F.

DIED ON THE FIELD OF HONOR

www.ingramcontent.com/pod-product-compliance
Lightning Source LLC
Chambersburg PA
CBHW080401170426
43193CB00016B/2786